The Bank of England: 1975-2025 The Economic Consequences for the People

Hector W. McNeill
SEEL-Systems Engineering Economics Lab
Portsmouth,
Hampshire, United Kingdom

Note

In terms of more detailed theoretical considerations, this publication is associated with an online working document entitled "Theories of Money".

This is in pdf format and can be accessed here:

http://www.boolean.org.uk/library/Theories_of_Money.pdf

This shows the transition from the Quantity Theory of Money (QTM) elaborated by Irving Fisher in 1911, through the Cambridge Equation, shaped by Arthur Pigou, Alfred Marshall and John Maynard Keynes in the 1920s and the author's Value Theory of Money (2020-2024).

HPC, 2021, ISBN: 978-0-907833-77-2

Date of publication: 2024
Hambrook Publishing Company
The publishing division of
The George Boole Foundation Limited

Contents

The Bank of England: 1975-2025 – The Economic Consequences for the People

Preface

Like all governments before them over the last 50 years, the current government has set out declaring its intention to achieve economic growth.

It is of course of vital importance to define the components that constitute growth that are relevant to Britain's current economic state.

After the 1939-1945 war, in the period 1945-1965, Britain experienced a high-growth period.

However, in 1966, Nicholas Kaldor, Professor of Economics at Cambridge University and leading adviser to the then Labour government, stated, in his inaugural lecture[1], that Britain did not have a sufficiently high rate of growth in productivity to be able to compete in the evolving international market. He advocated a more direct support for industry and manufacturing for the country to maintain innovation and productivity at adequate rates of advance.

It is now very evident that the failure to respond to this appeal has cost the country dearly.

---

[1] Kaldor, N., "*Causes of the Slow Rate of Economic Growth of the United Kingdom: An Inaugural Lecture*", Published: London; Cambridge University Press 1966.

Today, those countries that are focused on effective industrial and manufacturing strategies emphasizing productivity as opposed to monetary growth are those with the highest real growth and rising real incomes, including China, Singapore, South Korea and Taiwan. Japan has been undergoing difficulties as a result of monetary policy, and Germany is currently faltering as a result of an avoidable conflict, but until 2021, it had the highest balance of payments in the world.

Today China leads in terms of manufacturing and basic research on most modern technologies and has become the leading international benchmark for quality and prices of an increasing range of industrial and manufactured goods.

China's strategic vision with respect to the global south has been to establish its transport infrastructure (Belt and Road initiative), which will provide advancing logistics efficiency for expanding global trade.

With the post-1975 expansion of financialization associated with the petrodollar and globalization, growth became confused with Keynesian concepts of "aggregate demand" and monetarism's similar "money volume", while innovation and productivity were muffled by an increasing emphasis on profitability and shareholder value as opposed to being defined as real growth based on more for less[2].

---

[2] More for less is the nature of increasing productivity where the amount of resources required to create a unit of output falls as a result of a range of factors that contribute to rising productivity. See Annex 1, Productivity.

It is this basis for growth that is able to secure rising real incomes and the rising purchasing power of the pound.

As a result, within 58 years of Kaldor's appeal, we find ourselves with the second most negative balance of payments for industrial and manufactured goods on the planet, increasing income disparity, poverty and rising prices.

Rises in the prices of goods and services reduce the purchasing power of a given amount of money. If this sum of money is a person's disposable income, then rising prices reduce that person's real income.

Real incomes establish an individual's ability to engage in economic transactions to satisfy needs. Therefore, the relative movements of prices are important.

The entity nominally responsible for managing "price stability" through inflation control in the United Kingdom is the Bank of England, through its command over monetary policy decision-making.

This book reviews the impacts of monetary policy decisions taken by the Bank of England on the real incomes of constituents and covers the period 1975 to 2025.

Monetarism and monetary policy decisions have become more dominant in macroeconomic policy-making in the United Kingdom since 1975.

In terms of the country's international performance, the question becomes what is the connection between the Bank of England to our needed increases in innovation and productivity, and to industry and manufacturing in particular?

The mandate of the Bank makes no reference to any obligations that refer to innovation or productivity, or to industry and manufacturing but, rather, only a declared general objective of the Bank as being "price stability" for goods and services through the control of inflation by using variations in interest rates and to control the amount of money in the economy.

An excellent book by Harold James [3] covering a similar period deals with the wider considerations of national and international monetary policy management.

James refers to the Bank at the end of the 1970s as being:

"*deeply confused about its identity and quite inconstant in its performance.*"

This, I should interject, is after having been established in 1694 and having been in operation for over two and a half centuries!

Since 1975, under 11 Labour or Conservative governments and one coalition, there have been no comprehensive

---

[3] James, H., "*Making a Modern Central Bank – The Bank of England*", CUP, 2020.

industrial or manufacturing policies to encourage innovation and increased productivity. The alternatives to monetary policy decisions available under Keynesian and supply-side economics have failed to support sufficient innovation and rises in productivity as a result of technological change.

There have been ad hoc provisions, such as tax allowances and so-called "super-deductions" for types of investment, but these have not shifted the national productivity dial enough, if at all.

As a result, monetary policy has remained the only proactive policy left to manage the state of the economy, based on the general tenets of the Quantity Theory of Money (QTM).

This book identifies a series of problems of which most are aware but which politicians, government department spokespeople and the Bank of England have not been able to explain adequately or find solutions for. Invariably, there is a somewhat frustrating default state of affairs in which politicians and governments defer any explanations of economic issues to representatives of the Bank of England and, of late, increasingly to the Office of Budget Responsibility (OBR).

In the case of the Bank, when these are followed up, there is invariably no clarification as to why monetary policy decisions are often prejudicial to the real incomes of constituents. In its place, there is usually reference to the necessity to accept, unquestioned, monetary policy decisions because they are based on the principles on which monetary theory is based.

However, this is an unacceptable situation because changes in the relationship between the United Kingdom economy and the world economy have exposed the Quantity Theory of Money and monetary policy assumptions to be misleading, giving rise to erroneous policy decisions.

When questioned concerning relevant issues impacted by monetary decisions, such as productivity or income distribution, the default response by Bank representatives is that such matters do not fall within the Bank's mandate.

The economic policy domain in Britain has been so moribund and politics so unresponsive that such replies have never been followed up by governments to evaluate whether there is a need to establish a policy initiative to fill in an identified gap in the mandate of the Bank by other means. Of late, similar questions have arisen with respect to the scope and level of detail required in OBR "forecasts".

Note the growing tendency to assign policy decisions and responsibility to unelected technocrats, as opposed to elected politicians. As a result, such vital questions become water under the bridge.

The efficacy of monetary theory was undermined by the post-1973 growth in significant changes in the nature of international trade under rising petroleum prices followed by globalization and financialization. Post-1973, imported inflation associated with significant rises in the prices of petroleum and natural gas came to dominate the cause of inflation for something like 25 years in the last 50.

Such eventualities were never considered likely conditions for which Irving Fisher[4] had elaborated his Quantity Theory of Money in 1911. This is also true of a parallel, often cited statement made by Milton Friedman:

"Inflation is always and everywhere a monetary phenomenon in the sense that it is and can be produced only by a more rapid increase in the quantity of money than in output."[5]

Monetary theory and such a pronouncement became outdated as the international price of petroleum rose sevenfold between 1973 and 1983. The subsequent globalization and financialization resulted in a weakening of the effectiveness of national monetary policy with respect to inflation. This was because most inflation became the result of rising imported produce costs, as opposed to the volume of money in economies.

Following the OPEC price sanctions, the world underwent a period of stagflation, a combination of rising inflation and unemployment.

---

[4] Fisher, I., & Brown H.G., "The Purchasing Power of Money - Its determination and relation to credit interest and crises", Augustus M. Kelley, Publishers, 1911.

[5] Friedman, M., "*The Counter-Revolution in Monetary Theory*", *1970.*

As far back as 1975, the author observed that, in order to compensate for rising costs, companies raised their prices to maintain their profits to guarantee future activities and employment. This process, referred to as "anticipatory pricing", was also designed to ensure that companies accumulated sufficient cash flow to be able to afford the next period's inputs facing rising prices.

As a result, two important causes of inflation appeared, both of which were cost-push effects:

- imported (exogenous) input cost-related inflation
- domestic (endogenous) anticipatory pricing

Managing cost-push inflation

The impact of cost-push inflation is that it reduces the purchasing power of companies and individuals as a result of rising costs. However, the main policy instrument applied by the Bank of England has been to raise interest rates, which only exacerbates the situation by adding to costs and inflation.

In 1979, Nicholas Kaldor observed that a 3% rise in interest rates at that time would increase inflation by 2%.

Rather than tackle the root cause of inflation, the Bank of England substitutes a fall in real incomes due to inflation with a further reduction in real incomes as a result of rises in interest rates. Inflation eventually falls as a result of an imposed severe depression in real incomes or austerity.

The root cause of inflation

The balance of payments, the sterling exchange rate and inflation are all symptoms of a deficient growth rate in productivity. With an adequate rise in productivity, the balance of payments becomes positive as a result of import substitution and rising exports resulting from increasing competitivity of national production on international markets. As a result, there is a demand for sterling and the exchange rate remains robust. The inevitable result of rising productivity is a fall in inflation, from whatever cause, and in some product lines, falls in prices.

Productivity, economic theory and practice

A review of the main theories justifying policies and policy instruments, it is notable that in the foundation texts of Keynesianism, monetarism and supply-side economics the subject of productivity is covered by blank pages.

There is a parallel set of assumptions in Keynesian aggregate demand and monetarism's money volume, both assumed to generate demand and therefore economic growth.

But with a predominance of cost-push inflation, any such growth risks being undermined by inflation. The only solution is a macroeconomic policy that delivers a sustained rise in productivity.

Nothing in the Bank of England's mandate or in its policy instrument kit is meant to have any direct impact on productivity.

Because input prices were rising, to handle this input inflation, companies raised their prices to maintain their profits.

In the context of practical experience, and the current state of the world, monetary theory and pronouncements obscure the mechanisms that generate inflation, leading to perverse impacts on businesses and constituents. They remain the logic applied to decision analysis by the Bank of England. As a result, inappropriate policy instruments are used to control inflation, thereby imposing a significant trend in declining constituent real incomes.

It is notable that Harold James, in his book, also suggests that by the 2000s the Bank of England:

"*exemplified what was then thought to be best practice of a modern bank, running a clearly defined rules-based system around an inflation target.*"

However, it was during the 2000s and the post-2008 financial crisis and during the quantitative easing period starting in 2009 that other gaps were exposed in monetary theory, undermining the efficacy of monetary policy decisions. In particular, raising interest rates is not the right decision when facing cost-push inflation.

In spite of this, in June 2014, Andrew Bailey, Governor of the Bank of England, Christine Lagarde of the ECB and Jerome Powell of the Fed sat together on a stage and in a sort of mutual confidence-building effort and an attempt to gain credibility, each informed the public they were all doing the right thing in raising interest rates.

At a later date, Huw Pill, the Chief Economist of the Bank of England, informed the media that the constituents of the United Kingdom would have to accept the fact that they were poorer while remaining oblivious to the fact that the state of poverty and rising income disparity in this country is a direct consequence of inappropriate monetary policy decisions by the Bank.

Another factor complicating inflation control has been past international currency conflicts caused by competitive devaluations to boost exports. This is sometimes referred to as currency wars[6].

An inverse international currency conflict has seen the USA maintain high interest rates to attract capital, boosting the value of the dollar and exchange rate. Because of the dominance of the dollar in international trade, this has restricted the Bank of England's freedom, with the same objective of defending the pound, to lower interest rates.

This sort of impasse has been very evident in 2024, resulting in a major suppression of real incomes as a result of high interest rates in Britain impacting credit and mortgage payments, reducing the real incomes of most constituents.

---

[6] Rickards, J., "Currency Wars", Portfolio/Penguin, 2011.

The increasing application of financial sanctions by Britain and the USA on third countries, as well as sequestration of financial assets of other countries for political motives, has resulted in a significant loss of faith in US and British financial services and a rise in countries opting to use alternative or their own currencies to finance international trade.

This process, broadly referred to as de-dollarization, is likely to help other countries manage inflation better, and a side effect is already evident in a reduction in the use of the currently dominant currencies of the dollar, euro and pound in international transactions.

These changing states of affairs have required a completely different approach to inflation control, to which the Bank of England has yet to respond. As a result, over the last 50 years monetary policy, in spite of its mandate to ensure "price stability", the Bank of England has never been able to eliminate inflation, resulting in a pound devaluation treadmill and the tumbling real incomes of many.

The difficulty in completing long-run infrastructural projects such as HS2 is a result of the fact that budgets assigned to projects simply run out of purchasing power.

Over the last 50 years, we have witnessed inadequate investment and productivity gains in industry and manufacturing, a major deindustrialization, falling real incomes, rising income disparity and poverty where people in work cannot afford to purchase basic essentials, and we have a serious negative balance of payments in goods.

The reality is that governments and the economists advising them have failed to establish a policy framework geared to the promotion of innovation and productivity and have, by default, relied on monetary policy, which has no effect on innovation, productivity and growth. Monetary policy decisions have dominated economic management, while the Bank of England has no mandate to support these essential processes in industry and manufacturing in particular.

Explaining why economic theories, still taught in universities, are flawed is not a complicated task. But to be more productive, I present an alternative to the Quantity Theory of Money in the form of the Value Theory of Money[7]. Derived from this, I describe a practical policy solution to undo the range of monetary policy-induced impositions impacting businesses and the constituents of this country with a view to return the economy to a state of real sustainable growth in real incomes.

Central to this recovery is the question of productivity raised by Nicholas Kaldor some 58 years ago. Indeed, the common factor causing our declining balance of payments, inflation, the gradual fall in the exchange rate and constant decline in the purchasing power of the pound is inadequate productivity.

Many consider the whole concept of industrial and manufacturing policy to be "*dirigiste*" or a form of command

---

[7] For more details on the Value Theory of Money see the following document: http://www.boolean.org.uk/library/Theories_of_Money.pdf

and control attempting to choose winners. Such viewpoints seem to be based on a few past examples of attempts to establish industrial policies that were not successful. Industrial policy cannot be administered in a topdown fashion but needs to allow companies to adapt profitably to opportunities to invest and penetrate markets to benefit consumers with accessible real income-enhancing goods and services.

Over the period 1975 to date, the ***Real Incomes Approach to Economics*** or ***Real Incomes Objective (RIO)*** has emerged as a distinct approach to economics as a result of analysis and development that I have undertaken.

This approach can reverse declines in the balance of payments, lower inflation, gain control over the exchange rate and stabilize or even increase the value of the pound and real incomes because it is designed to sustain incentives for innovation and productivity increases, which reduce unit costs.

The only way to measure the effectiveness of any policies designed to lower inflation is to measure the policy's impact on real incomes. If a policy raises real incomes, it is solving the problem. If it further reduces real incomes, as is common, the policy is a failure.

This focus helps transfer returns to investment from an emphasis on rentier and financialized activities and the low income services sector to a concentration on higher real returns in industry and manufacturing.

Observing the application of the Bank of England's policy instruments, such as interest rates to tackle inflation, it becomes apparent that this often substitutes the fall in real incomes due to inflation with a continued fall in real incomes due to raised interest rates or taxes.

In other words, the Bank of England does not in reality solve the critical impact of inflation but, rather, imposes a form of debilitating austerity that depresses markets, causing price depression in parallel with real income declines.

A specific real incomes policy proposed is ***Price Performance Policy (3P),*** a general macroeconomic policy which is neither sector-specific nor does it attempt to identify "winners". It is not an industrial policy because it benefits all sectors by raising real incomes and reducing inflation through an incentive for a sustained rise in productivity and price constraints.

Besides being distinct from Keynesianism, monetarism and supply-side economics, RIO and 3P constitute a new branch of constitutional economics that ensures that economic policies applied within a constitutional framework support the interests of the state, society, economic units and the individual.

Here, "interest", in each case, is defined as the level of real income.

In line with the general notions of promoting freedom, RIO and 3P aim to assist individuals in pursuing their own objectives to raise their real incomes while preventing such pursuits from imposing constraints on others.

This approach has the general objective of replacing zero-sum transactions where degrees of unfairness prevail to create transactions in support of a ***positive systemic consistency*** in which transactions are characterized by mutual benefit and more representative of a state of enhanced natural justice.

While many would assume that imposing social concerns on strictly economic and financial decisions would result in inefficiency and waste, the reality is that this approach can create a far more competitive and efficient real growth economy than anything thus far witnessed.

What does become apparent is that the usually unstated role of the Bank of England to monitor the exchange rate of the pound and the balance of payments, as fundamental factors in the standing of the British economy, is a real but very different concern to that of ensuring an affordable cost of living by raising the real incomes of constituents.

It is here that we encounter diametrically opposed objectives according to the interests of the wage-earning public and those whose operations and interests lie more directly in transacting financial and physical assets, as well as the management of transactions affected by the exchange rate.

There is a systemic monetary policy failure embedded in monetary theory and derived practice that imposes bouts of austerity on the part of wage-earning constituents, while

those concerned with assets and finance are far less affected, if at all.
Recommendations for changes to aspects of the current mandate of the Bank of England necessary to enable a recovery of the economy are made because at the moment, the Bank of England cannot satisfy both the exchange rate and balance of payments status without imposing prejudice on constituents because its policy instruments have no substantive impact on productivity and competitivity.

This book is divided into the following general sections:

1. The confused student
2. An attempt at harnessing innovation
3. The consolidation of cost-push inflation
4. Monetary mechanism outcomes
5. Real Incomes theory and policy
6. Why RIO is a new supply side paradigm
7. Implementing a Price Performance Policy

1. The confused student

I was first introduced to economics around 1964 while studying agriculture at Cambridge University. I then completed a post-graduation in agricultural economics in 1966/1967, which included completing macroeconomics and microeconomics at the Faculty of Economics and an excellent applied course in "Project Evaluation" based on World Bank case studies.

At the School of Agriculture, this was complemented by courses in biometry, policy design and a dissertation concerning the operation of international commodity control schemes.

Part of my undergraduate training included the planning of operational farms including poor units, average-sized family farms and corporate farms, based on the linear programming algorithm and using very detailed statistics on farm productivity according to variable input combinations supporting each of the farm's animal or crop production lines.

This data came from detailed, regularly updated annual sample surveys of types and sizes (areas) of farms throughout the UK, although I only worked on data collected in East Anglia by the School of Agriculture's Farm Economics Branch on behalf of the National Agricultural Advisory Service (NAAS).

As a basic practical guide to identifying where any specific farm could improve productivity and therefore income and profits, survey results contained a range of levels of achievable productivity associated with different combinations of variable[8] inputs classified as poor, average and good practice for every line of animal and crop production.

Individual farm plans were drawn up to sustain an advance in productivity in the sector. Where a plan included an improved level of practice, the farmer would receive advice on the requirements in terms of changes in inputs.

As a result, I had a good applied and practical appreciation of how businesses set prices and why they might raise their prices or even lower them. Above all, I had a good understanding of the changes companies need to introduce to remain profitable.

Monetarism

At the Faculty of Economics, lectures on "monetary policy" sought to explain that as the volume of money in the economy rose either through the government borrowing money and paying for economic activities or simply companies and individuals taking out loans from banks, the effect would be a rise in unit prices of goods and services.

From my agricultural training, I knew that there was no obvious relationship between the volume of money in the economy and the prices at which farmers would attempt to sell their produce. Farmers raising their prices were likely

---

[8] Variable inputs vary with the scale of production so if a crop required 125 kilos of fertilizer per hectare, 10 ha. of that crop would require 1.25 tonnes of fertilizer.

not to sell their produce when another farmer was charging less on the day.

Farmers, like other businesses in competition and those operating at the leading edge of productivity in any given year, would be able to make more aggregate profit by even selling at a lower price in comparison with farmers not at the leading edge of productivity.

My question therefore became:

"*What is the mechanism that causes businesses in competition to raise their prices simply because there is more money in the economy*?"

I asked a lecturer and subsequently professors and other lecturers that very question.

The Quantity Theory

The first person I asked, a lecturer, grabbed a chalk and on a blackboard wrote out the following[9]:

$$M.V = P.Y$$

Stating that the relationship between money volumes (M) and average prices of goods and services (P) was to be

---

[9] This identity or formula was first created by Irving Fisher, of Harvard University, in 1911. Fisher, I., & Brown H.G., "*The Purchasing Power of Money - Its determination and relation to credit interest and crises*", Augustus M. Kelley, Publishers, 1911.

explained by this relationship known as "The Quantity Theory of Money".

The periods "." in this formula represent a multiplication sign "x". He then added that "V" referred to the velocity of circulation of money, or the number of times money circulated through transactions, and "Y" refers to the quantity of goods and services purchased at that average price "P".

Since Y is the total sum of goods and services purchased under a given volume of money "M", this is also referred to as "real income" or what people got for the money spent. Having seen this formula or identity in previous lectures, I realized that I had not been provided with an answer to my question.

Inflation

I was being told that the cause of rising prices of goods and services, or inflation, was proportional to the volume of money M in the economy. However, that simple statement provided no explanation of how that change in prices takes place. Why do prices rise? What was the mechanism? I therefore repeated my question pointing at the "M" and asking why, if M is increased, it is assumed that the average prices "P" of companies in competition and producing goods and services will increase?

I then explained my reasoning as being that because any company raising prices would lose market share, there was no reason why they would. There was no logical incentive to do so.

I again asked, "What is the mechanism that translates higher money volumes "M" into higher average prices "P""? I asked this question of several lecturers and professors at Cambridge and later at Stanford University Department of Economics 1967 to 1969 and always received the same answer. Each person addressed would either refer me to the "Quantity Theory" or, according to the location, write the Quantity Theory on a black, green or white board as if that was the explanation.

None was able to explain the mechanism.

From my past direct and practical involvement in farm planning and knowing the differences between poor, average and good practice, and from conversations with farmers, I knew that, in general, companies would only raise their prices as a result of rises in the prices of their inputs, or their costs, in the form of such things as land rent, seeds, animal feed concentrates, fertilizer, etc.

Milton "explains"

Around 1975, I happened to chance upon a television interview of Milton

Friedman, who at that time was promoting a "*New Monetarism*", and I was intrigued when the interviewer asked him the very same question.
I imagined that, at last, I would hear the answer to my question. To my surprise, Milton Friedman was unable to provide a clear explanation of any mechanism. However, under the interviewer's persistence, Friedman became

somewhat irritated and asserted, "*It happens in the long run*!" which, of course, is not a mechanism.

What I found to be paradoxical was that Friedman had become well known, by then, for his statement:

"*Inflation is always and everywhere a monetary phenomenon in the sense that it is and can be produced only by a more rapid increase in the quantity of money than in output.*"[10]

And yet in 1975, he was unable to explain why this was the case.

This impasse became, for me, a disappointment and I dubbed this as "*Friedman's dilemma*", which I would have to solve myself.

I have to admit that this sealed my cynicism of the value of the Quantity Theory of Money because it is impossible by studying such a simple formula to work out why money volumes generate inflation in the unit prices of competing companies.

Stagflation

In 1973, OPEC raised petroleum prices as a sanction against those countries who had sided with or assisted Israel in several conflicts over the Palestine question; most were petroleum importers.

---

[10] Friedman, M., "*The Counter-Revolution in Monetary Theory*", *1970.*

Petroleum prices rose sevenfold in the following decade. This steep rise in costs resulted in most countries facing the combination of inflation with a subsequent rise in unemployment, known as slumpflation or stagflation.

I felt that I was adequately qualified to work out a policy solution to the rising stagflation.

I was in Brazil at the time.

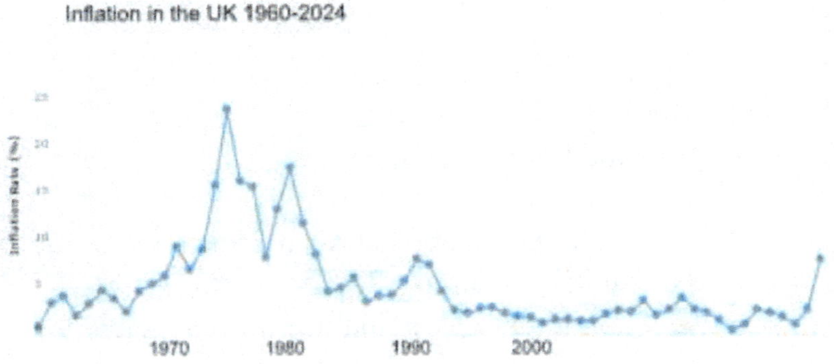

International petroleum prices 1950-2024

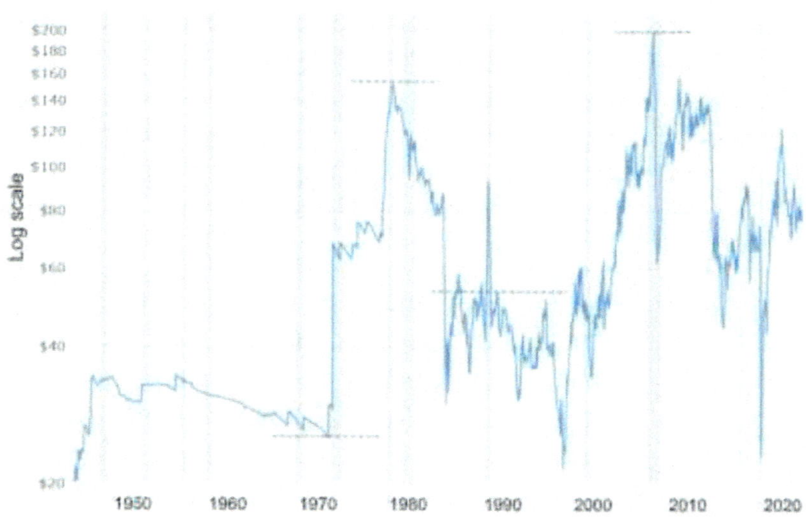

I attempted to assess the effectiveness of all the existing policy instruments, such as monetary expansion and contraction, interest rates, government borrowing and taxation, to control inflation in the prices of goods and services, i.e. to lower it.
No matter how hard I tried, I found that it was impossible to lower inflation without imposing prejudice on constituents. In other words, existing Keynesian and monetarist policy instruments proved to be ineffective.

I found this to be quite frustrating, given that I had qualified in economics at two universities well known for their economics training. There were plainly gaps in the instruction received.

The Quantity Theory of Money and inflation

The assumption under the Quantity Theory is that a growth in the money supply creates demand and therefore economic growth. On the other hand, the QTM indicates that a rise in money volume results in inflation. In other words, it is assumed that additional money creates too much demand, resulting in what is referred to as "demand-pull" inflation.

Milton Friedman qualified this by stating that inflation is caused by a more rapid rise in money volume relative to output.

However, with the OPEC-induced stagflation, the cause of inflation was not too much money (M) in the economy or related to output and/or demand, but rather it was caused by the rising input prices of petroleum. Therefore, the cause of inflation was companies having to respond to rises in their input costs to maintain their profits, thereby generating "cost-push" inflation.

Petroleum and cost-push inflation

Most only consider petroleum and natural gas to be inputs to generate energy and power for industry and households as well as lubricants, fuel oil, diesel, gasoline and aviation fuel for transport.

However, petroleum and natural gas have something like an additional 6,000 derivatives and petrochemicals covering a vast array of products and applications including bitumen, waterproof sheeting, fertilizers, herbicides, fungicides, a vast range of types of plastics and composites and many other products used by most sectors in the economy. The prices of these derivatives accompany the baseline prices of petroleum and natural gas on the international markets, creating a broad front of cost-push inflation throughout the economy.

Anticipatory pricing

One of the notable behaviours of companies in Brazil in 1975 was that, as their input prices rose, companies responded by raising their output prices in order to maintain their profits to guarantee future activities and employment. This is not an imaginary phenomenon but was the general reality. I discussed this at length with many businessmen at the time, and this process of ***anticipatory pricing*** was considered to be the main survival mechanism for business under the prevailing cost-push inflation impacting input prices.

This practice was also designed to ensure that company cash flow grew sufficiently to be able to pay for the input requirements for the next production period, whose prices were rising.

Because managers did not want to be short of funds, when paying for the next period's inputs, there was a natural tendency, in the name of caution and risk aversion, for companies to overestimate the likely rise in costs, and this resulted in inflation increasing steadily from 1975 through the 1980s and 1990s, pushing Brazil close to hyperinflation largely as the result of anticipatory pricing.

Brazilian inflation rate following prolonged period of anticipatory pricing

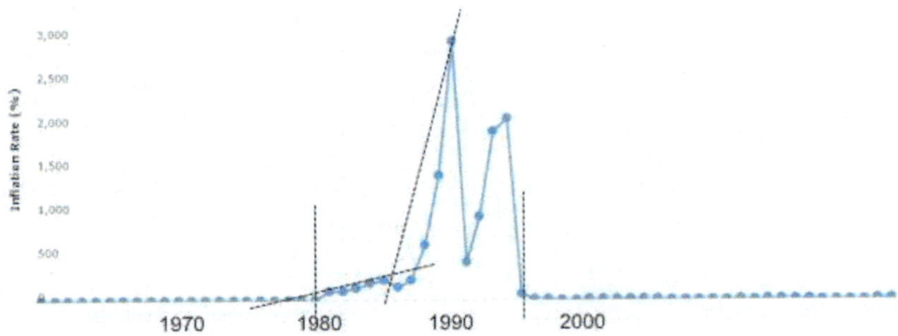

Today, the practice of anticipatory pricing appears to have recently been rediscovered by academic economists[11], who now refer to this as "sellers' inflation" or even "greed-flation".

The Quantity Theory of Money and policy

As we know, the Quantity Theory assumes that inflation is the result of there being too much money (M) in the economy and that inflation is caused by demand-pull. However, as can be appreciated, the Quantity Theory does not provide any insights as to the effect of the reality of rising input prices (production costs).

Because the assumption is that inflation is demand-pull, the policy instruments of monetarism are limited to the application of higher interest rates and taxation as ways to reduce "demand" or the volume of disposable money (M) to

---

[11] Weber, I., "*Sellers Inflation - Is inflation just a number game or does it hold deeper societal implications?",* New Economic Thinking

reduce inflation. However, the only solution to rising costs was to substitute petroleum and its derivatives, as well as to change technologies to reduce unit costs by raising productivity.

But, since inflation was caused by a cost-push effect of rising petroleum prices between 1973 and 1983 (a sevenfold increase over that period), the application of interest rates and taxation in an attempt to lower inflation turned out to be a failure; they were and remain the wrong policy instruments under cost-push circumstances.

This is why, in 1975, I could not find a policy framework to control inflation using conventional policy instruments without prejudicing constituents.

Taxation

Raising taxes reduces disposable incomes and net profits, so the overall effect is a fall in real disposable incomes and a fall in consumption or demand.

In the case of companies producing goods and services, a lower throughput caused by a fall in consumption results in corporate fixed overheads rising per unit of output. As a consequence, this increases cost-push inflationary pressure. At the same time, higher tax reduces net profits, encouraging companies to respond by applying anticipatory pricing more intensively, thereby resulting in rising inflation.

In the case of households, higher taxation reduces net disposable incomes so as to reduce purchasing power, resulting in a lower real income and consumption. As can be fully appreciated, the use of taxation to control inflation in this way only prejudices companies and households.

The Supply-Side Economics approach

About the same time as my own work was taking shape as RIO-Real Incomes Objective economics, Robert Mundell, a Canadian economist, was perfecting what came to be known as "*Supply-Side Economics*" (SSE), which was based on a novel taxation approach that, rather than raise taxation, provided lower marginal taxation for higher income earners.

The theoretical justification was that this should lead to more money being available to invest in productivity enhancing changes, resulting in an eventual reduction in inflation due to lower output prices.

SSE seems to be a logical theory, but in practice, such incentives become giveaways with no guarantee that the benefits gained by higher-income earners would be spent as imagined by policymakers. The adoption of this policy as part of President Reagan's counter-inflationary policies did not result in the expected levels of investment but served to increase income disparity. It would have been more effective to apply the tax variations to corporate taxation as opposed to high-income earners, as will be explained in Part 4 of this book.

In addition, the lower tax take resulted in a mounting government deficit impacting social programmes upporting low-income segments of the population.[12]

SSE, or Reaganomics, as it was referred to, was also called "*Trickle-down economics*". A significant part of the failure of this policy, like a parallel initiative undertaken by the Thatcher government in the United Kingdom, was the use of exceedingly high interest rates to tackle what was a cost-push stagflation.

Interest rates

Traditionally, interest rates are used to attract capital to British banks when the exchange rate was falling and imports were becoming more expensive during inflationary periods. However, in the case of inflation following the OPEC petroleum crisis in 1973, the cause of inflation was cost-push, so raising interest rates only raised input costs and cost-push inflation, encouraging companies to indulge in anticipatory pricing and creating yet more inflation.

Increasing interest rates lowers the ability of households to maintain their rates of consumption by reducing their purchasing power and lowering their real incomes.

---

[12] Roberts, P. C., "*The Supply-Side Revolution*", Harvard University Press, 1984. [12] Kaldor, N., Lord, "*The economic consequences of Mrs. Thatcher*", Duckworth, 1983.

Indeed, in 1979, when confronted by the Thatcher government proposals on monetary policy to apply interest rate rises to reduce inflation, [12] Nicholas Kaldor estimated that for each 3% rise in interest rates, there would be a 2% rise in inflation. It is remarkable how such a stark reality expressed by a competent economist could be ignored.

The Quantity Theory of Money was prejudicial

We therefore have to conclude that the circumstance facing the United Kingdom, for some 20 years between 1973 and 1993, was inflation caused by the cost-push effect of petroleum and petroleum derivative prices.

Therefore, the logic of the Quantity Theory of Money and the policy actions applied in the form of the instruments of taxation and interest rates only made the circumstances for producers and consumers of goods and services worse.

The Thatcher government, ignoring Nicholas Kaldor's advice but following Milton Friedman's advice, proceeded to intensify monetarist solutions to cost-push inflation by raising interest rates. Friedman suggested that the economy would then return to its "natural" equilibrium position.

In discussing this with Robert Neild [13] of Cambridge University on television, Friedman was unable to explain how the economy would return to this "equilibrium". For

---

[13] Neild, R., "*The 1981 statement by 364 economists*", Chapter 1 in "*Expansionary Fiscal Contraction*", CUP, 2014.

some time, Nicholas Kaldor had been explaining that there was no real equilibrium when there was growth and even less so when this was combined with rising productivity.

One result of this decision was the repossession of 600,000 homes of people who had entered into mortgage contracts in good faith but whose lives were disrupted and prejudiced as a direct result of completely inappropriate monetary policy decisions rendering such people incapable of paying their premiums while receiving no compensation for the damage imposed by policy.

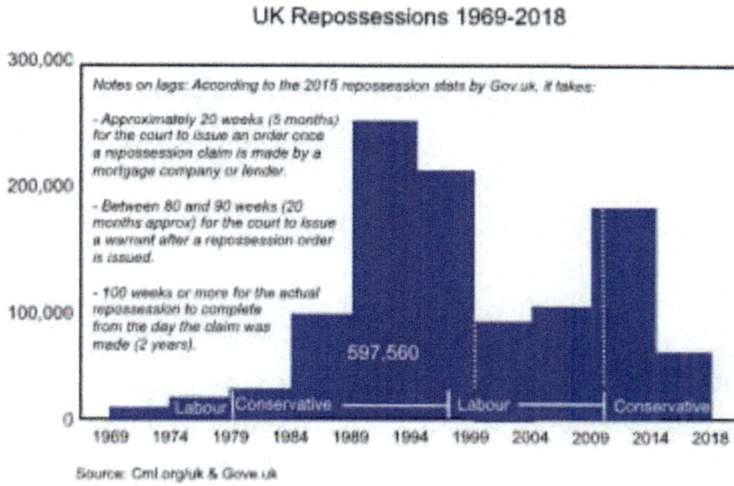

This was the result of an imposed reduction in real incomes or purchasing power caused by arbitrary and significant rises in interest rates raising credit and mortgage premiums.

Why are monetary policy decisions arbitrary?

As described by the constitutional economist James Buchanan [14], constitutional economics includes the democratic process of identification and a shared agreement on a moral form of behaviour to support the interests of the state, society and the individual, and confirmed through public choice.

The public goods of laws and regulations are an important means of recording and preserving such moral decisions and make up the fundamental components of the structure of constitutions, which should last several generations.

It is a rational expectation that all matters involving the concerns and needs of constituents should be subject to public review to facilitate an exploration of options to identify and agree on the most appropriate actions to satisfy needs through public choice.

The case of repossessions of houses from families who have taken out mortgages in good faith only to have their ability to repay the mortgage undermined as a direct result of monetary policy decisions is the result of an arbitrary act transgressing the constitutional economic principles of supporting the interests of society and individuals.

Inflation's main impact is to reduce the purchasing power and real incomes of constituents. However, raising interest rates does not reduce inflation but contributes to the further

---

[14] McNeill, H. W, "*The importance of Constitutional Economics*", Real Incomes Approach, 2012

reduction in the purchasing power and real incomes of constituents.

Therefore, the policy decision is arbitrary because it does not reduce inflation but creates the externality of accelerating loss of real incomes; no regard is paid to constituent needs.

Monetary policy and public choice

The United Kingdom gained universal suffrage in 1928.

In anticipation of this important development, changes in the management of monetary policy had taken place. These were designed as an attempt to remove all aspects of monetarism or monetary policy from review and consideration by the public through public choice.

The basis for this statement is presented by Clara E. Mattei in her book, "*The Capital Order*"[15], and in particular in Chapter 6, entitled, "*Austerity, a British Story*". In this section, Mattei describes the proceedings/exchanges of participants in the 1922 Genoa Economic and Financial Conference in which particular attention is given to the declarations of the British participants associated with the Bank of England.

In summary, the conclusion, in light of what have become the eventual facts on the ground, is that monetary policy decisions should not rest with politicians but rather with technocrats operating from within an independent institution.

---

15 Clara E. Mattei, "The Capital Order" 480 pages The University of Chicago Press, 2022

In the case of the United Kingdom, the institution concerned is the Bank of England.

Mattei refers to the influence of Ralph Hawtrey, a UK Treasury official who, according to papers and statements produced in the 1920s, sought to distance any monetary decisions from public choice by a process of depoliticization consisting of the following components or tenets:

- removing the state from economic relations;
- removing economic policies from democratic decision-making;
- understanding or promoting economic theory as apolitical.

Austerity was a key component of adjusting things like balance of payments in goods, the exchange rate and as an element of controlling inflation, based on the additional tenet or way to address these issues, "*produce more and consume less*".

This default to austerity can be related to a sharecropper economy arrangement mentality. When there was a bad harvest year, the sharecropper and his family were expected to face the consequences and to produce more and consume less.

In the early days of industrial growth and manufacturing, a good deal of inputs was made up of labour deployed in labour-intensive tasks, so "*produce more and consume less*" was a form of appeal for higher labour output but without the necessary investment to lever labour input through advances in technology to gain higher productivity. Therefore, austerity became a self-defeating tactic in its failure to lay the foundation for sustained rises in productivity. In place of this, the expectation was more hours on lower real wages.

An example of this approach enduring into the 21st Century can be recognized in the experience of Yanis Varoufakis as a new Minister of Finance for Greece during the Greek debt crisis. In response to the suggestion that an election had taken place and therefore issues needed to be reviewed, he described the reaction of the German Finance Minister[16], Wolfgang Schäuble, in the statement that, '*Elections cannot be allowed to change economic policy.*'

Policy is normally established by the will of representative governments, and in cases where the policy is clearly prejudicing a group of constituents, it would be normal to renegotiate the policy so as to correct such a situation. Although, perhaps, Schäuble was referring to undertakings associated with loans to Greece, and although they are contractual, it is reasonable to assume that since Greece was suffering unexpected hardship, rational adjustments should have been introduced.

In any agreement, each side needs to ascertain risks by carrying out due diligence, but the problem is that the constituents (voters) were never involved, only politicians

---

[16] Varoufakis, Y., "*Wolfgang Schäuble (1943-2023)*" at www.yanisvaoufakis.eu

and creditors. Therefore, in reality, this was not done, so, in the case of Greece, to satisfy creditors, productive assets were sold off and the people paid the price.

UK Corp

In the case of monetary policy decisions in the United Kingdom, as can be readily appreciated, the workforce that made up the majority of consumers, as voting constituents, was the human segment required to "consume less" and tighten their belts as and when policymakers would require increases in output. This general approach saw the economy being managed as if constituents were the workforce of a conglomerate, managed by unelected technocrats acting as executives.

This logic was originally applied to sustain a positive or balanced balance of payments and a stable exchange rate related mainly to goods. On the other hand, it was also this austerity-related policy that doubled up as the measure assumed to represent the cure for inflation in the prices of goods and services.

This reality raises a question concerning the actual degrees of freedom constituents have to pursue their objectives.

For whose benefit?

While there has been an attempt to minimise public discourse on monetary policy design and decisions within the framework of a democratic society, it is worth assessing whether or not this basis for monetary operations makes any sense in terms of the economy or the population in a country with universal suffrage.

Through the constitutional economic lens, this includes the assessment of monetary policy's contribution to the interests of the state, society, economic units and the individual.

There are possible interpretations of justifications for this position of distancing monetary policy and decisions from popular scrutiny and public choice.

One is a logical professional concern that those with little experience in what financiers consider to be an esoteric subject that requires some expertise should only be managed by those with adequate understanding and experience so as to avoid mistakes.

The argument here is that such a basis for operation is to lower the risks associated with decisions and to ensure economic stability.

On the other hand, there is also the possible interpretation that this barring of the involvement of representatives of constituents, politicians, from any involvement in decisions, albeit in a subtle manner, is related to the creation of an operation that benefits financiers or some other specific interest groups.

In terms of natural justice or fairness of treatment of constituents, it is a valid legal concept and a specific procedural right to counter bias. Natural justice has provided a means for victims to receive fair treatment, and this featured in the early English constitutional documents via Edward Coke and others in the 17th Century[17].

It is clear that while an attempt is made to distance monetary policy from politics, surely such theorists do not, by the same token, suggest monetary policy is above the law?

The evidence

To evaluate these justifications, two forms of evidence can be used to decide whether the current basis for the operation of monetary policy is acceptable.

One is to review the logic of the theory of money, which for more than a century has been based on the Quantity Theory of Money proposed by the Harvard University economist Irving Fisher[18] in 1911, and to compare what this theoretical identity predicts as outcomes of monetary policy decisions with what has transpired.

The second basis is simply to observe the general performance of the economy under monetarism since the 1920s, which would have to include the 1929 New York Stock Exchange Crash and the ensuing Depression. The most interesting period to observe the impact of monetary policy on the relative wellbeing of constituents is, however, the last

---

[17] Coke, E., "*Institutes of the Lawes of England*" (1628-1644)

[18] Fisher, I., & Brown H.G., "*The Purchasing Power of Money - Its determination and relation to credit interest and crises*", Augustus M.

Kelley, Publishers, 1911r

50 years, following monetarism becoming the dominant factor in UK macroeconomic policy in 1975[19].

The post-1975 period to date has been one of significant transformation, including a major deindustrialization of the British economy, the loss of skilled industrial and manufacturing jobs and growth in the services sector.

In evaluating either the monetary theory or actual performance of the economy, we are concerned to see to what extent evidence supports the assertion that economic and monetary decisions have been taken in the interests of the state, society, economic units and individuals and have avoided creating differentiations or arbitrary benefits to one set of economic actors over others.

If the latter is true, then this would render the current basis for operations unacceptable and in need of an altered theoretical and/or policy practice, probably raising questions as to the mandate and policy instruments used by the Bank of England.

Different schools of thought but a common thread

The baseline logic of monetarism in relation to inflation is summarized in the Quantity Theory of Money (QTM).

The associated logic of the QTM is that by increasing money volumes, there is an increase in demand and this results in

---

[19] Denis Healey, Moran, J., "Denis Healey agrees to the demands of the IMF", FT, Sept 4, 2010.

economic growth and a rise or maintenance of employment levels.

This can be recognized in both Keynesianism (debt-based government borrowing stated to maintain or create employment) and monetarism (private debt-based monetary advances stated to generate demand and growth) as equivalent aggregate demand or money volume approaches respectively.

The counter-inflationary policy decisions in the fiscal domain follow the same logic of altering aggregate net disposable incomes by increasing taxation to exert control over inflation and unemployment.

Governments and the common macroeconomic approach to economics dealing with aggregates of highly heterogeneous populations of sector participants and constituents, take decisions based on observing trends in aggregates.

One of the main effects of declining productivity is a fall in the balance of payments for goods because national output is not internationally competitive.

Investment and rentier money therefore tends to move away from financial intermediaries in the United Kingdom, causing a dearth of available investment funds. As a result, demand for pounds declines and the exchange rate moves against the pound, reflecting its declining value.

The normal corrective response is for the Bank of England to raise base interest rates to attract funds in search of returns in an act termed to "strengthen the pound". Notice that this is the initial step to attempt to prevent a decline in the balance of payments and value of the pound.

The problem is that raising the value of the pound only makes British produce for export more expensive for potential importers.

Therefore, notice that the cause of the balance of payments problem is an inadequate level of productivity or competitive prices, and the conventional solution does not solve the issue of competitivity, since with a "stronger" pound, productivity needs to rise even further for products and services to remain competitive.

In the meantime, whereas raising interest rates might "strengthen" the pound, these same interest rate rises prejudice both consumers and business by causing outstanding loans such as consumer and capital equipment finance or home mortgages to rise, creating an additional erosion in real incomes on top of the erosion caused by inflation.

Therefore, the notion that austerity or "producing more and consuming less" as a corrective measure is as illogical as it is highly prejudicial. What is needed are sustained increases in productivity so that consumption can rise on a basis of lower priced output stimulating exports and thereby strengthening the value of the pound.

The Monetary Policy Decision Cycle (MPDC)

The Bank of England's monetary policy decisions on interest rates and government decisions on tax vary over typical monetary policy decision cycles (MPDC) according to the state of inflation.

The Quantity Theory of Money (QTM) would suggest that as money volumes increase, so will the prices of goods and services, and when money volumes are reduced, the prices of goods and services will decline.

So monetary policy decisions are essentially an attempt to stimulate growth with money supply incentivized through low interest rates and taxation, and then, when inflation in goods and service prices reaches some critical point, it is reduced by increasing interest rates and taxation.

This sequence of events can lead to a misinterpretation of money supply in the sense that a considerable amount of investment and growth is generated from investments, where most of the funds are drawn from company cash flow. This investment, therefore, remains free of the influence of interest rates. As a result, the majority of activity giving rise to real growth is not related to advances made by banks as some function of interest rates.

Therefore, there is no direct relationship between interest rates and growth because the growth comes from the activity of investment, which is normally generated by company cash flow.

Components of the Monetary Policy Decision Cycle (MPDC)

Sequence	Inflation Status	Policy Response			
		Base rate	Taxation	Money Supply	Objective
1	Low	Low	Lower	Rising	"Growth"
2	Rising	Raise	Raise	Risng	Reduce Inflation
3	High	Raise	Raise	Frozen	Reduce Inflation
4	Falling	High	High	Falling	Reduce Inflation

The demand-pull illusion

Therefore, the QTM gives the impression that average prices of goods and services rise with money volume or aggregate demand, leading to growth. To counter inflation, it is necessary to reduce demand by reducing the volume of money in the economy.

Therefore, the operative mechanism for driving the economy is assumed to be what is referred to as "***demand-pull***".

The question is why should competing companies producing goods and services raise their prices because M rises if doing so would result in them losing market share?

The cost-push reality

With financial deregulation and many new financial derivative products taking shape, private banking activities have shifted from their primary policy role as mainstream lenders in support of farms, SMEs, businesses and households to trading activities carried out largely for the benefit of bank shareholders and executives.

This growth in activity directs a considerable amount of money into assets, exacerbating the cost-push situation where such assets become inputs to the production of goods and services.

Quantitative easing

In 2009, with the economy suffering from a severe fall in aggregate demand following the global financial crisis, the Bank of England introduced a new monetary policy tool called 'quantitative easing'. The policy involved the Bank of England creating new money to purchase government bonds on the open market. Its aim was to inject liquidity into the economy, which the Bank believed would have beneficial effects. These include lowering interest rates, increasing lending and boosting investment.

A Select Committee report

In 2021, the House of Lords Select Committee on Economic Affairs published a report[20], after taking evidence on the impacts of QE, entitled:

"*Quantitative easing: a dangerous addiction?*"

This title suggests that the evidence provided by the Bank of England and others was far from convincing; thus, the question as to whether quantitative easing is no more than a dangerous addiction remained as part of the report title.

---

20 Economic Affairs Committee, "*Quantitative easing: a dangerous addiction?*", Parliament Website 16 July 2021

The Governor of the Bank of England, Andrew Bailey, objected to the title of the report, suggesting that the word addiction has a very damaging and particular meaning to many people who are suffering.

People suffering? People suffering as a result of monetary policy decisions was of course a matter for concern, but since monetary policy is supposed to be apolitical and policy preferences and decisions are to have no reference to the preferences of the electorate, Bailey's comment revealed a sensitivity to a usually hidden fact that monetary policy impacts the wellbeing of constituents and they have no say over its form or function.

This focused the spotlight on monetary policy, in contrast to Hawtrey's position, as being a highly political issue.

The Select Committee concluded:

In spite of the evidence provided, the Committee considered quantitative easing's precise effect on inflation to be unclear.

A notable but largely ignored contribution to the evidence provided to the Committee included the statement,

"*Quantitative Easing is a policy with no theory*".

The Bernanke Report

In May 2024, Ben Bernanke, the past Governor of the Federal Reserve Bank of the USA, submitted his report[21] following his assessment of the Bank of England's procedures and methods in forecasting.

The report was quite devastating as it associated Britain's central bank with amateurism and guesswork being exercised with inadequate models. It seems that the Bank is certainly not an establishment that possesses the most sophisticated determinate decision analysis models to guide decisions, in spite of having been in the business for over 300 years.

It is very evident that with a sound decision analysis model, most of what is contained in this book would have been self evident in the data.

But given Bernanke's findings, this is of no surprise.

Ukraine

In a demonstration of a fatal separation of UK government strategies in economics, security and foreign policy, since 2022, we have witnessed another petroleum and natural gas price crisis with the Ukrainian civil war having become a major confrontation.

---

[21] Bernanke, B., "*Forecasting for monetary policy making and communication at the Bank of England: a review*" Bank of England, 2024

This war was avoidable, but there remains a separation of strategic security policy decisions on the part of the UK government from national economic risk analysis considerations concerning the potential strategic economic security impacts on the national economy and constituents of the country. As a result, we have witnessed a rise in energy prices, a massive rise in cost-push inflation and, as in the 1970s and through the 1990s, the incorrect policy instruments being applied to lower inflation of what is a cost-push inflation. Accordingly, for something like 25 of the last 50 years, we have seen the Bank of England, in such cases, applying the wrong policy instruments to lower inflation.

Economic prejudice

As a result, the average and projected inflation over the period 2022 through end of 2024 (estimated) led to direct economic costs to the economy as a loss in real incomes of around £300 billion. The direct cause was the energy price crisis and raised inflation directly associated with foreign policy and security decisions in relation to Ukraine.

Analysis of the Quantitative Easing (QE) effect

During the initial low base interest rate and low taxation phase of the monetary policy decision cycle that was experienced during quantitative easing following the 2008 financial crisis, initially the prices of goods and services did not rise. On the other hand, all asset prices rose substantially and almost immediately. This was because banks were applying cheap money to purchase assets on their own accounts or through loans to corporations. Three asset classes in particular were early participants in bank dealings:

- Land
- Buildings (real estate)
- Commodity positions

These were converted into input costs via "asset & commodity services"[22] in the form of prices and rental of land for agriculture and other projects. The same applies to buildings (real estate) as prices and rental of commercial offices, warehouses, industrial units, offices, logistics infrastructures as inputs to supply-side goods and service companies, as well as housing for consumers.

Because the assets of land and buildings are serviced through rental or sales, they usually operate on the basis of fixed-term contracts (rental and/or finance for purchase), the introduction of higher prices to the goods and services markets and households as input costs to business and households tend to occur sometime after the initial rise in money volumes, and asset price rises, varying between 12 months to 24 months after the original rise in asset prices.

The commodity positions include futures contracts and other forms of trading including food, fibre and feedstocks (biofuels), hydrocarbon-based products including petroleum, gas, fuel oil, diesel, gasoline and aviation fuel. Some 6,000

---

[22] Commodity services include: trading in any commodity, including money on the basis of arbitrage and speculation through overnight and futures contracts. Commodities include just about anything but include hydrocarbon energy products (petroleum and natural gas) and their derivatives, mainly different classes of fuel, and over 6,000 additional products. Other commodities include food, fibre and feedstocks.

petroleum derivatives used in most sectors (including fertilizer and plastics) have been the cause of imported inflation (exogenous inflation) for around 25 years of the past 50 years associated with conflicts.

Friedman's dilemma solved

This simple fact explains the "mechanism" that, as a student, I was seeking. This is also the solution to "*Friedman's dilemma*" as to why inflation occurs "*in the long run*" after money volumes rise.

Therefore, the principal cause of inflation in goods and service prices is the result of companies responding to the rises in input costs, ***a cost-push effect*** of inflated assets (land, buildings and commodities). It is not directly related to demand-pull for goods and services.

Since the assumption of the QTM monetary policy logic is that money volume demand-pull causes inflation in goods and services, it becomes apparent that reducing money volumes will not affect this type of inflation.

Thus, while asset price rises are directly linked to money volume and demand, asset prices subsequently become the main sources of cost-push inflation in goods and service production.

2.An attempt at harnessing innovation

1945-1965, When things seemed to work

After the Great Depression that followed the New York Stock Exchange Crash of 1929, public works programmes organized under the New Deal initiatives in the USA provided a demonstration of the role of government investment in reducing unemployment through public works and general economic development initiatives.

It would seem to be only natural that this would become a new approach to macroeconomic policy. John Maynard Keynes elaborated on this realization in his book, *"The General Theory of Employment, Interest and Money"*[23], where in order to maintain "full employment", the solution proposed was for governments to borrow money and spend it on public works and infrastructure to generate jobs.

Following the Bretton Woods Agreement in 1944, which brought the world economy back onto the Gold Standard based on the US dollar as the world reserve currency, the period 1945-1965 in the United Kingdom was considered to be a "Golden Age of Capitalism" while Keynesian economists considered Keynesianism to provide the foundation for a better run economy.

However, Robin Matthews, a Cambridge economist and

---

[23] Keynes, J. M., "*The General Theory of Employment, Interest and Money*", Palgrave Macmillan, 1936.

Keynesian, completed a study of the performance of the British economy over the period 1945-1965[24] to find that although investment and productivity growth raised real incomes, reduced income disparity and meant people on average wages could afford by buy a house, no Keynesian policies were applied because throughout this period there was full employment.

In fact, the balance was positive throughout the period and monetary policy was deflationary with relatively high interest rates.

What is important to note here is that there was a good deal of investment, which rather than coming from banks, came from corporate cash flow, and operational price setting fell well within the bounds of accessibility of the population's purchasing power.

It would seem that this growth was largely driven by a spontaneous rise in investment and productivity unrelated to any specific policy.

The most significant element of this growth in real incomes is that nominal incomes rose in an environment of competitive prices, signifying that productivity was rising at an adequate rate to ensure competitive prices were profitable. It would seem that in this period there was little cost-push inflation or anticipatory pricing.

---

[24] Matthews, R. C., "*Why Has Britain Had Full Employment Since the War?"* Economic Journal, September, 1968.

Nicholas Kaldor and productivity

In parallel with this range of developments, Nicholas Kaldor did not consider the rise in British industrial productivity to have been high enough, and he provided an explanation as to why the United Kingdom needed to support industry and manufacturing in the future to ensure a robust national growth and maintenance of higher real incomes [25] in an increasingly competitive world economy.

His explanation was relatively simple in that the activities of designing products and processes and producing products maintain a constant flow of innovation and improvements that support the creation of equipment, products and devices that contribute to the productivity of all sectors of the economy. So, his 1966 lecture referred to the importance of securing a sustained national diffusion of innovation in the form of advancing technologies.

If policy permitted any decline in industrial innovation and technical advance, Kaldor advised that Britain would lose its place in the ranking of competitive economies and gravitate towards an inability to import-substitute or export more to maintain a positive balance of payments in goods.

---

[25] Kaldor, N., *"Causes of the Slow Rate of Economic Growth of the United Kingdom: An Inaugural Lecture"*, Inaugural lectures, University of Cambridge, Cambridge University Press, 1966.

An evolving Labour party

In the lead up to this statement, important shifts in socialist outlook were championed by Hugh Gaitskell, the Labour party leader, and Anthony Crosland, a Labour MP. In 1959, Gaitskell had attempted to change party policy on nationalization (Clause IV).

The intellectual justification for his stand was to be found in work by Anthony Crosland in his book[26], *The Future of Socialism* published in 1956. Here, he argued that there was no need for nationalization because the actual power resided in the management of economic activities and not in the hands of the owners and the state could influence sector activities sufficiently well. This particular observation was to become the central justification for reducing the force and significance of Clause IV.

More remarkable is the fact that Crosland is reported to have observed that capitalism seemed to have solved the problem of coming up with adequate per capita incomes for the workforce.

Crosland's observations can be traced back to meetings of the Congress for Cultural Freedom (CCF)[27], launched in 1950 in Berlin and headed by Melvin Lasky. The general

---

[26] Crosland, A., "*The Future of Socialism*", Jonathan Cape, 1956.

[27] *"How the CIA Took the Teeth Out of Socialism",* Fletcher, R., WCM
Library. originally published in Philip Agee and Louis Wolf, eds, "*Dirty Work: the CIA in Western Europe*", Zed Press, 1978 pp 188-200.

drift of the content of Crosland's book had been discussed at a Milan CCF conference attended by Hugh Gaitskell, Denis Healey, Rita Hinden and Daniel Bell. The latter was the author of a book[28] in the same vein entitled, *The End of Ideology*.

There are sound arguments for considering Anthony Crosland to have laid much of the intellectual foundation for what was to be picked up, some 20 years later, as New Labour policy under Blair.

After 12 years of Conservative governance, in October 1963 the Labour leader Harold Wilson warned his audience[29] that if the country was to prosper, a "new Britain" would need to be forged in the "white heat" of the "scientific revolution" for industry to drive economic progress. This was a reaction to a view promoted by C. P. Snow[30] that British social and political elites were dominated by "natural Luddites", whose ignorance of science and engineering made them singularly unfit to govern a world in which technology was becoming ever more important. This was also referred to at the time as the "Two cultures" debate.

---

[28] Bell, D., "*The End of Ideology: On the Exhaustion of Political Ideas in the Fifties*", Harvard University Press, 1965.

[29] British Library, *"Harold Wilson's 1963 pledge to harness the white heat of a scientific revolution"*, 2023.

[30] Snow, C. P., *"The Two Cultures"*, CUP, 1965.

Labour went on to win the 1964 election.

Following the advice of Kaldor, this Labour administration did set out to introduce a more innovative basis for Britain's economic growth to establish a basis for a future role for Britain in an increasingly competitive world. There was an attempt, at least in declared objectives, to marshal the power of increased technological productivity to accelerate the development of the British economy for the coming period. They attempted to address a broad set of issues considered to be holding Britain back.

In 1965, Anthony Crosland introduced his Circular 10/65 to transform public education into a comprehensive education system. He thought this would become an agent for social mobility.

Jennie Lee, a Labour MP, presented a White Paper on the proposition of an Open University, which would require no formal qualifications for entry. She faced significant pressure from other MPs against this project, but she had the tenacity to push through, with Wilson's help, the formation of the Open University by 1969. The Open University "of the air" became the largest university in the world, creating opportunities for millions of people worldwide, including corporate executives who otherwise would not have benefitted from this unique system.

This Labour administration, with the NHS purchasing coming under state control, questioned the ethical basis for pharmaceutical products being profit-based.

However, in spite of plans to apply this more innovative approach to a Labour administration which would last 15 years (1964-1979), any such efforts were to be rudely interrupted by the development of events in the Middle East, stagflation and the debilitating growth of financialization.

The OPEC petroleum price sanctions had the effect of giving rise to cancellations of orders for the Concorde airplane whose budget, like the TSR-2, the world-leading British supersonic strike and reconnaissance aircraft developed in the 1950s and 1960s, ballooned to unsustainable levels in terms of cost-benefit.

Kaldor's approach to innovation and productivity development as a basis for growth was more practical and was not based on such ambitious "mission-based growth". In the two examples failure, in the end, was related to not having the financial means and the budget running out of control resulting in cancellations (TSR-2) and not having done enough homework concerning the factors that would limit the market for Concorde.

There was, in spite of C. P. Snow's, "Two cultures" concept a problem with associating innovations with science and basic research and boffins as opposed to more rapidly deliverable technological systems feeding of multiple branches of science through product and process design based on systems engineering principles.

Wilson's referral to the "White heat of the scientific revolution" would perhaps have sounded more convincing if he had substituted the world "scientific" with "technological" or from a fund of theory to something of practical use.

3. The consolidation of cost-push inflation

Financialization

While the details of money theories are of significance because these affect the logic of policy decisions at the national level, far more significant changes took place on a global level, which in turn affected national economic performance.

In 1973 following various military conflicts between Israel and Arab countries over the issue of the treatment of Palestine and Palestinians, OPEC imposed price sanctions by raising petroleum prices to punish those who had supported Israel in military events over the Palestinian question, most of whom were petroleum importers.

Petroleum prices rose seven-fold over the subsequent decade, throwing the world economy into turmoil.

The subsequent response, in terms of economic policies, was an acceleration in the movement towards financialization.

What is financialization?

Financialization is the process whereby all economic considerations are reduced to a nominal financial quantification while the vital considerations of innovation, productivity and changes in technology and technique became secondary to short-term profit maximization. This reduced business strategies from an emphasis on competitivity of products and services to managing assets and resources to maximize profits.

The crucial problem with financialization is that what appear to be distinct policies or even schools of thought, such as Keynesianism or monetarism, and supply-side economics, are in fact questions of emphasis regarding which aspect of financialization is more significant as a policy target. Thus, there is Keynesian aggregate demand (expressed as a quantified monetary aggregate) or monetarism's money supply (expressed as a quantified monetary aggregate) and the status of the economy expressed in the form of aggregate GDP.

Increasingly, economic activities have involved so-called financial engineering where the manipulation of numbers substitutes for applying physical technologies or even productivity in real goods and services production. Business incomes increasingly were made up from the holding of assets, which generate an income from those who make use of the asset. This created a major financial services activity that is made up of über-rentiers.

Although many see this evolution as recent, it had already been detected before the Great Depression and, indeed, was to a large extent the cause of the Great Depression, and the crises in the post-1970s period and now. The American economist, Thorstein Veblen,[31] wrote the following in 1921:

"*Half a century ago it was still possible to construe the average business manager in industry as an agent occupied with the superintendence of the mechanical processes*

[31] Russet, C. E., "*Darwin in America – The Intellectual Response 18551912", Freeman, 1976.*

involved in the production of goods and services. But in the later development the connection between the business manager and the mechanical processes, has on average, grown more remote; so much so, that his superintendence of the plant or of the processes is frequently visible only to the scientific imagination... His superintendence is a superintendence of the pecuniary affairs of the concern, rather than of the industrial plant; especially is this true in the higher development of the modern captain of industry."

Veblen considered this evolution to be associated with a change in motivation that brought to the fore financial manipulators, who sabotage and retard, rather than advance technological development. He considered success in this business world to wait on guile:

"*The successful man under this state of things succeeds because he is by native gift or by training suited to this situation of petty intrigue and nugatory subtleties. To survive in the business sense of the word, he must prove himself a serviceable member of this guild of municipal diplomats who patiently wait on the chance of getting something for nothing; he can enter this guild of waiters on the still-born pecuniary gain, only through such apprenticeship as will prove his fitness. To be acceptable, he must be reliable, conciliatory, conservative, secretive, patient, and prehensile.*"

So, well before the first major financial crisis in the last century, Veblen had described the specific changes that would give rise to such a crisis. Because nothing in macroeconomic theory has sought to address these issues, the schools of economic thought failed to tackle such basic flaws so as not to disagree with those who dominate the "pecuniary" affairs of the economy and who continue to promote increased financialization.

It is understandable why Thorstein Veblen's seminal works are not widely taught in our schools of economics.

Thorstein Veblen pointed out the drift from an emphasis on physical processes to one of financial processes. The subsequent evolution of economics saw macroeconomic schools embedding the very same negative evolution by giving increasing emphasis to nominal financial aggregates and paying far less attention to innovation, technology, technique, learning and production performance at the microeconomic level. Indeed, chairs in economics have been endowed at many universities by the organizations that Veblen criticized, creating a tendency for an enhanced emphasis on financialization. This problem of bypassing technology and innovation created a form of technological ignorance on the part of many macroeconomic theorists.[32]

Veblen lamented the fact that economics was not an evolutionary science.

Clearly, proposals for growth and escaping from the excessive debt generated by over-financialization are not going to come from Keynesians, monetarists or supply-side

---

[32] McNeill, H. W., "*On the Problem of Technological Ignorance amongst KM Economists'*, Charter House Essays in Political Economy, 1981.

economists because a cursory review of the foundation texts of these approaches possess very little of practical use on the application of innovation and essential technological change to secure rises in productivity.

By default, Keynesianism, monetarism and supply-side economics all lack any substantive references to the importance of innovation and technical change and therefore make no provisions and/or possess no adequate tools in their policy tool kits to encourage innovation and technological change geared to increasing productivity.

In terms of attracting investment or equity capital, there used to be attention paid to a company's prospects and price-earnings ratios to determine whether it was worth investing in them. In the past, this was often determined by the degree to which a company was innovating and investing in leading-edge technologies or announcing new and significant contracts and undertakings to generate more profit and returns by producing better competitively priced goods.

With financialization, share buybacks have been used to raise share values and benefit selected shareholders. During quantitative easing, starting in 2009, 50% of the rise in the share index in London attributable to share buybacks.

Growth depends upon market penetration of competitively priced goods and services and this also depends upon higher productivity and improving quality of output.

However, what came to be referred to as shareholder value became a comparative measure of corporate success and performance.

In that race, the existing corporate accounting norms and corporate taxation of gross profits saw an emphasis on margins, profits and dividends as well as executive bonuses linked to changes in shareholder value as opposed to improvements in physical productivity and wage settlements.

One reason for this is that the classifications of corporate accounts items place labour in the "costs" category, while shareholder dividends come out of profits, as does tax.

As a result, over time, the proportion of GDP made up of profits has grown faster than the proportion of GDP in wages.

Since the workforce makes up the majority of the consumers, this form of financialization results in demand arising from aggregate wages being impacted by gradually higher prices and therefore a reduction in real incomes and real growth. In place of competitive unit prices creating rising real incomes for consumers and the workforce, there are many examples of the negative impacts of financialization.

For example, in the medical insurance sector in the USA, the establishment of legislation supporting Pharmacy Benefit

Management (PBMs) companies[33] as separate units from medical insurance companies is designed to avoid a 15/85 (profit/costs) split imposed by medical coverage regulations. These units demand rebates from pharmaceutical companies and then pass on the product to be listed at heavily elevated prices.

Examples exist of the mark-ups being as high as 1000% generating a high profit for the insurance companies while the patients pay these high prices, meaning that the insurance contribution is in fact close to zero because the patients have already paid the whole real cost. Thus, PBMs and another similar setup Group Purchasing Organizations (GPOs) extract value without adding any at all and radically reduce the real incomes of consumers.

How did the OPEC 1973 decision intensify financialization?

Johannes Witteveen, a Dutch politician, became the Managing Director of the International Monetary Fund in 1973, just as the OPEC international petroleum price crisis began. Since the IMF had been formed to manage the international aspects of currency exchange rates under the gold standard, which was abandoned in 1971, many doubted that the IMF had a future.

The petroleum crisis created the conditions of stagflation, which combined rising inflation and unemployment.

---

[33] Inside China Business: "*High prices for Ozempic and Wegovy , two European-made weight-loss drugs, expose or corrupted system.*"

Rapidly falling productivity because of rapidly rising costs and falling earnings stalled investment and reduced the ability to generate profits.

Presidents Nixon and Ford urged Witteveen to criticize OPEC. However, Witteveen avoided following this advice, probably because he was dealing with Arab countries and because he himself went by the name of Murshid Karimbakhsh and was a Sufi Muslim.

The Petrodollar

Witteveen, sought to solve the ensuing financial crisis by encouraging mainly Islamic OPEC members to lend parts of their rising dollar accumulations to the IMF, who in turn would lend these funds to developing countries to be able to afford to purchase petroleum which faced constantly rising prices.

These funds, which later were also used to create sovereign wealth funds, also created investment flows and purchases in the West and mainly the USA.

For developing countries, the IMF set up loans, using Arab finance, so that lower income countries could purchase their petroleum requirements. Although this was promoted as the IMF "helping" oil-consuming nations pay for their petroleum imports and sustaining world trade, this move very much favoured the expansion of OPEC Middle Eastern oil producers' sales at rising prices, so the flow of oil at increasingly high prices continued.

Financed imports paid interest on these loans and thereby raised their cost to low-income countries.

By various means, the IMF became increasingly involved in the use of petroleum export-generated funds raising the loans issued by the IMF seven-fold over the period from 1973 to 1977 (from less than $1 billion to around $7 billion).

In reality, the proportion of such recycling handled by the IMF was relatively small, and private institutions took over this Petrodollar process acclaimed as an example of international cooperation.

This was celebrated in a formal agreement between the USA and Saudi Arabia in 1974, in which a secret clause referred to Saudi Arabia purchasing Federal bonds. This 50year secret agreement meant that the USA was not particularly concerned about the rising price of petroleum impacting the rest of the world.

In 2024, this agreement terminated, raising questions as to the future of the petrodollar.

Going in the wrong direction

While providing "finance" during the stagflation period, the IMF did nothing to effectively tackle inflation and productivity because they encouraged both austerity and the incorrect application of raised interest rates to tackle inflation in an expanding cost-push inflation world. The result was the increase in international debt in low income countries.

The abandonment of Keynesianism

In 1975, not knowing how to handle the slumpflation crisis created by the OPEC decisions, the Labour government's Chancellor Denis Healey abandoned any Keynesian perspective with a budget that substituted full employment and demand with the balance of payments as the policy target while also:

- Setting cash limits on government programs, except social programs
- Reduced public spending where it was deemed not to be unmeasurably beneficial
- Made income policy voluntary, knowing this would result in a decline in the standard of living

This decision was precipitated as a result of the Treasury overestimating the borrowing requirement of the government. Fearing a "run on the pound", Denis Healey requested a loan from the International Monetary Fund (IMF).

It was very unusual for a developed nation to make such a request to the IMF. Having said that, the IMF had recently advanced loans to Hungary, Latvia and Iceland. However, the UK was another thing altogether. In the case of the United Kingdom, Johannes Witteveen took personal control of these negotiations in London concerning the conditions. Witteveen encouraged the British Government to impose an increased austerity by intensifying the conditions already set by Healey.

It is notable that Germany and France resisted taking a similar route.

The Germans had a better appreciation of what was at stake, namely supply-side productivity. Based on a centuries-long tradition of apprenticeships and technical education, Germany's rising balance of payments was the result of a massive accumulation of tacit knowledge and a flow of technological innovation managed by a very large number of SMEs.

The more academic British educational system and the combination of some governments with a more visceral approach to industrial relations and the human resources skill base (tacit knowledge)[34] led to insufficient consideration being given to incentives to encourage technological and human resources investment. Labour had understood this, giving rise to educational initiatives but the OPEC sanctions disrupted this initiative

Spreading the word – International Development

The fact that Healey had made the balance of payments a policy target had a reinforcing effect on this aspect of IMF thinking and policy. Delighted with having managed a loan to the UK, making the balance of payments the main policy target was a feather in Witteveen's cap. He authorized the publication of a book in 1977, entitled, *The Monetary Approach to the Balance of Payments*[35] by the IMF. Typical

---

[34] Tacit knowledge- see Annex 1 Productivity

[35] IMF, "*The Monetary Approach to the Balance of Payments*", International Monetary Fund, 1977.

of IMF publications, this consists of a series of very academic papers by IMF staff members based on a mass of statistics and simple mathematical formulae which discuss the relationships between monetary policy and the balance of payments. There is no reference to the real economy or the specific conditions within the supply-side goods production sectors that, in themselves, can improve the balance of payments situation on a sustained basis by increasing productivity.

As in the case of Milton Friedman's assertions on cause and effect, the papers in this publication constituted an inadequate approach to the balance of payments because there were no auxiliary policy actions identified and designed to encourage rises in productivity, such as was the case in Germany. As a result, the status of real wages and therefore aggregate demand, was entirely dependent upon centralized diktats, which only look at the balance of payments in a vacuum, or in monetary balance terms.

The IMF always insisted on the same austerity policies associated with loans to low-income countries, which confuse productivity with budgetary cost-cutting exercises while denying the necessary actions to raise productivity, resulting in raised debt and with any growth through productivity being virtually impossible.

The book does not consider the main contributing factors to the balance of payments equilibrium to be gained through increased productivity and therefore the contributions fail to provide any practical indications as to the options for policy incentives to bring about beneficial change.

There was a failure to address the petroleum and hydrocarbon consumption issues that arose in the 1970s. This required an expansion in petroleum substitution technologies, but the monetary approach led to an expansion in the power and financial interventions of OPEC countries, and in particular Saudi Arabia's worldwide expansion of financial and political influence.

Labour party splits

This experience of imposed austerity caused the Labour government to begin to split into a social democratic and a socialist camp, leading to disagreements with the trade unions and the onset of a loss of industrial productivity and employment.

It is thought that this "sterling crisis" contributed to the Conservative victory in 1979.

Productivity agreements were abandoned, and the UK returned to the politics of wage-earner austerity shakedowns for the sake of the balance of payments. This failed because nothing was done to address productivity; the point emphasized by Nicholas Kaldor.

The fact that such conditions were agreed with Britain was considered to be a confirmation of the global importance of the IMF. In spite of the fact that very little of this loan from the IMF was used and it was paid back within a short period, this bolstering of confidence of the logic of the IMF's "recovery" policies applied in Britain encouraged them to repeat this ineffective and prejudicial approach throughout the world in advanced, transitional and low income economies alike.

The problem was that having considered stagflation and a declining balance of payments to be a monetary phenomenon, the broadening range of credit for petroleum consumers meant the efforts to substitute petroleum with more technical alternatives or to advance the necessary research to identify solutions were put off, essentially for about 30 years.

As a result, the period 1975 through to 2021 saw a rise in the indebtedness of low-income countries and a rise in the intensity of greenhouse gas emissions and pollution associated with the use of petroleum and petroleum derivatives.

This consolidated the cost-push nature of global inflation.

Politics

There does not appear to have been any analysis of the degree to which Witteveen's assistance to the petroleum exporting countries in supporting their campaign to punish countries who supported Israel in the Israeli-Palestinian conflict was, in reality, a Muslim assisting Islamic nations. Or was it simply that his status as a monetary economist was sufficient to write off this calamity as a misguided judgement on international finance?

It is doubtful if anyone knows what Witteveen's inner motivations were, but his decisions, although appearing to be helpful and well-meaning at the outset, set in train policy transitions and spheres of influence that have not been positive.

There was a slowdown in the necessary transitions in technology and a continued absence of productivity incentives in macroeconomic policy. Little effort was made to reduce the inordinate financial power of petroleum exporters. Now, some 50 years after turning petroleum into a political weapon, they still remain fully capable of inflicting the same sorts of damage on importing nations at their will.

It is notable that when Witteveen passed away in 2019 at the age of 97, the first organization to publicize his death was the website of the Sufi Muslim organization.

Sovereign Wealth Funds

As a result of the accumulation of funds by petroleum exporters, they were in a position to create large Sovereign Wealth Funds to be used as sources of funds to invest in ventures considered to be for the national benefit.

The leading sovereign wealth funds have holdings worth between $500 billion and $1.75 trillion each.

NYMEX-New York Mercantile Exchange and the Petrodollar

On the initiative of a few insistent individuals, The New York Mercantile Exchange (NYMEX)[36] ended up taking over international trading for petroleum and the Petrodollar.

[36] McGrath Goodman, L., "*The Asylum – The Renegades Who Hijacked the World's Oil Market*" W. M. Morrow, 2011.

Brokers and traders made multi-million-dollar commissions and this Petrodollar flood spread into commodity futures and international financial trading and even derivatives.

In 1972, Black and Scholes[37] developed a hedging model designed to reduce the risks associated with financial instrument options or derivatives where Petrodollars helped drive what became known as a Grey Derivatives market to reach the dimensions of national economies while remaining distant from any effective financial authority oversight.

The Black-Scholes Model was computer based, and computer-based trading expanded into a range of trading techniques including high-velocity trades, where such volumes of money could be used to drive up asset prices or even to depress prices through false trades (giving the appearance of purchasing intent, to build up market expectations, then cancelling to shave off a margin).

Hedge Funds

Several hedge funds were spin-offs from trading activities such as petroleum dealing at NYMEX. These saw the size of financial resources involved in trading, not only financial instruments, but also whole companies with some emphasis on asset-stripping and then maximization of profit by discarding less profitable segments including workforces. Very little attention was paid to innovation, technical change and productivity.

---

[37] Black, F. & Scholes, M., "*The Pricing of Options and Corporate Liabilities*", Journal of Political Economy, 1973. Also referred to as the "Black–Scholes options pricing model".

The leading 20 hedge funds have financial assets of between $35 billion and £150 billion each.

Globalization

The impact of OPEC price sanctions on productivity in the UK was drastic and as a result between 1973 through to the present date there was an expansion of offshore investment to geographic areas with lower labour costs such as South East Asia. The impact of this was the inverse of that promoted by Nicholas Kaldor as a requirement for Britain's future growth. This involved investing overseas as opposed to investing in British companies operating within the country, leading to a decline in adequate investment and, as a result, inadequate growth in productivity in industry and manufacturing.

The Onshore Engineering Club

In 1990 there was a rise in unemployment in the UK and the author carried out a survey on behalf of the UK Government's Manpower Services Commission of 100 high-tech companies in the County of Hampshire to enquire about their interest in contributing to the creation of an "*Onshore Engineering Club*". The intent was to create a foundation hub for the identification of those techniques and technologies that could re-initiate a reversal of the offshore engineering trend to expand British industry and manufacturing within the country on an increasingly competitive basis along the lines achieved by Germany.

German industry had not only remained at the leading edge of engineering technology but for 50 years had implemented

a cheap energy strategy through long-term contracts with Russia in exchange for the manufacture of the pipeline. This was intensified after 1970 with additional long-term contracts associated with additional pipelines under "Ostpolitik".
Whereas US policy increasingly attempted to discourage Germany from following this policy, the reality was that many US and European firms had joint ventures with Soviet and post-Soviet firms as set out in "Vodka-Cola"[38].

As far as the Offshore Engineering Club survey went, only one firm requested a follow-up, and on arrival at the firm, located in Havant, the person concerned had no idea of the reason for the meeting and had no authority to discuss or decide on such a question.

Most firms seemed to have seen their future in not investing in Britain.

The consequences of financialization, cost-push inflation, flawed monetary theory and practice

Our State of Economic Affairs

The combination of offshore investment and inappropriate monetary policies in the United Kingdom after 1975 with policy based on the logic of the Quantity Theory of Money (QTM), the Bank of England and the government used just two (2) policy variables to manage the economy in the form

---

[38] Levinson, C., *"Vodka-Cola"*, Gorden-Creminesi, 1979.

of base interest rates and taxation, while also using government borrowing to fund activity.

As a result, from 1975 to 2024, with no industrial or manufacturing policy and with only inappropriate policy tools combined with an inadequate theory of money to guide monetary policy decisions, the British economy has suffered from the following general problems.

Internal account

- Inadequate supply-side investment
- Inadequate rises in supply-side productivity
- A major deindustrialization
- Loss of worker tacit knowledge (de-skilling)
- Loss of product and process design capabilities
- Loss of domestic sources of innovation
- A policy failure to eliminate inflation
- A failure to secure a policy objective of price stability
- A failure to prevent a constant decline in the value of the pound
- Loss of higher paid skilled jobs
- A significant rise in the "valuation" of assets
- A constant decline in real wages and household purchasing power
- Rising income disparity between asset holders and wage-earners
- Rising poverty (people in work unable to afford basic essentials)
- Gradual decline in growth rate

External account

- Declining competitiveness of goods and rising negative balance of payments in goods
- Services sector has some export potential to balance external account but largely low income with high income occupations facing erosion from digital technologies and AI
- Declining ability to import substitute increasing transfer of funds to offshore producers
- The second most negative balance of payments for goods on the planet

Analysing cost-push inflation

In 1975, in initiating the work that gave rise to this book, I observed anticipatory pricing in Brazil, justified as a logical financial corporate management procedural response to cost-push inflation. However, I also noted that anticipatory pricing tended to increase cost-push inflationary pressure to the extent that later it ended up accumulating into hyperinflation.

Following a prolonged period of globalization and financialization, anticipatory pricing has been rediscovered in the form of "seller's inflation"[39] or even "greed-flation" where profits are considered by many academics to have increased excessively.

The result of anticipatory pricing, as a common practice when companies facing cost-push inflation, ends up making

[39] Weber, I. M., "*Taking Aim at Sellers' Inflation*", Project Syndicate, July 13, 2023

cost-push inflation a general condition facing goods and services sectors both in business-to-business as well as business-to-consumer transactions.

The result of the emphasis on shareholder value contributed to the rise and impact of anticipatory pricing and cost-push inflation.

How companies influence inflation

Observing anticipatory pricing in 1975 in Brazil, I realized that this was a common practice in all economies when faced with cost-push inflation.

Therefore, in terms of seeking to design a counter inflationary policy it is useful to understand to what degree companies contribute to inflation in their operations to identify the nature of the required changes in operations for companies to increase their productivity to set prices to secure real growth by reducing or eliminating inflation.

Components of prices and price rises

Unit Prices (UP) are composed of Aggregate Unit Costs (AUP) and the Margin applied (M).

AUC can be broken down into three main contributing cost components: Variables[40] (V), Labour (L) and Energy (E).

---

[40] Variable inputs vary in proportion to the scale of production, so energy E is also a variable whereas Labour (L) is often considered to be overhead.

So, AUC = V + L + E

Therefore, prices will tend to rise in response to any rises in variable cost components, labour wages and/or energy prices.

In the 1970s through 1980s the main cost rise was associated with energy price rises and the rises in petroleum derivatives which followed the petroleum price.

Organizational productivity[41]

Any rise in unit prices in response to aggregate unit costs is seldom a linear response because decisions can be made concerning short-term resource allocation and adjustments that alter the productivity of the process concerned in the short term without any investment. The capital-disembodied productivity arises from the use of resource allocation algorithms such as linear programming. On the other hand, rises in productivity rising from capital-embodied productivity involves additional investment.[42]

---

[41] Organizational productivity is the resultant productivity of a company related to capital-embodied productivity. Capital disembodied productivity (including explicit knowledge) and Labour tacit knowledge

[42] Further information on capital-disembodied and capital-embodied productivity see Annex 1.

The Price Performance Ratio (PPR)

In order to measure the contribution of each company to inflation I devised a coefficient known as the Price Performance Ratio (PPR)[43]. This is measured by comparing the unit output percentage price change in response to the percentage change in aggregate unit costs of inputs.

Thus:

PPR = %UP/%AUC

Where

%UP is the percentage change in output prices;
%AUC is the percentage change in aggregate unit costs;

Besides measuring the contribution of companies to inflation, the PPR is also a measure of the effectiveness of corporate actions in applying productivity to minimize the divergence between input and output inflation.

---

[43] McNeill, H. W., *"Price performance Fiscal Policy – A Real Incomes Approach",* INTERCOMEX, Rio de Janeiro, 1976.This version applied to rising inflation only. In 1981 Robin Matthews, Professor of Political Economy at Cambridge University, on reading a monograph (McNeill, H. W., *"Price Performance Fiscal Policy – A Real Incomes Approach"*, Charter House Essays in Political Economy, HPC, 1981) concerning 3P advised me to add the condition for deflation, which I undertook, transforming 3P into a general macroeconomic policy, as opposed to a specific counter inflationary policy. In a computer this is handled by simple Boolean decision trees

PPR ranges have break points, which provide useful information.

These are shown in the table below.

Relationship of anticipatory pricing to the PPR ranges and associated indicators

PPR	Anticipatory Pricing?	Profit Rate	Output Inflation	Currency Value	Consumer Real Incomes
> 1.00	Yes	Rises	Above Input	Falls	Falls
= 1.00	Yes	Remains	= to Input	Falls	Falls
< 1.00	No	Falls	Under Input	Rises	Rises

There are three basic PPR scenarios:

PPRs that exceed unity (>1.00) raise inflation above the input rate and depreciate the value of the currency, thereby reducing consumer real income;

PPRs of unity (=1.00) indicate inflation remains at the input rate while the currency and real incomes of consumers lose value;
PPRs of less than unity (<1.00) reduce inflation and raise the relative value [44] of the currency and real incomes of consumers.

[44] Relative value rises in comparison to the other cases of PPR equal to or greater than unity.

Conclusion

In terms of the real incomes of constituents as consumers, the beneficial state coincides with PPR values that are less than unity. However, this also coincides with the situation where companies end up with lower profits.

Why monetary policy fails

As explained in previous sections, most inflation in goods and services has its origin in cost-push inflation as an initial response to rising land, real estate and commodity price position rises and then this is generalized by anticipatory pricing to become a general cause of inflation.

The logic of the Quantity Theory of Money (QTM) assumes that inflation in goods and services is caused by excessive money in the economy or demand-pull and therefore to control inflation the monetary policy cycle switches to raised interest rates accompanied by government raising taxation rates to reduce the level of disposable incomes in the economy (M).

As can be readily appreciated, the actual policy instruments applied under monetarism following the logic of the QTM end up generating inappropriate impacts because the attempt to reduce inflation uses means which actually increase inflation and reduces real incomes because costs are raised.

Therefore, the current monetary policy instrument of interest rates is as inappropriate as taxation.

Interest rates and taxation are an exceptionally ineffective and inefficient way to reduce inflation because they undermine the real income status of both companies and households.

The natural response of companies in the form of anticipatory pricing exacerbates the situation of consumer purchasing power.

RIO-Real Incomes Objective

The outlook, however, is not that bleak.

In the Preface of this book, I referred to the Real Incomes Approach to Economics, also known as RIO-Real Incomes Objective economics. As a branch of constitutional economic analysis, this provides an alternative and convenient approach upon which to evaluate monetary policy outcomes.

Such an assessment reviews the degree to which the policy outcomes satisfy the constitutional requirements of supporting the interests of the state, society, economic units and individuals.

In this context, it is necessary to consider the implications of having one central bank which controls monetary policy for four quite different countries, England, Scotland, Wales and Northern Ireland each with different economic structures and histories.

An assessment of monetary policy decisions in the context of RIO and this constitutional reality, is a judgement of the degree to which outcomes achieve a ***positive systemic consistency.***

In order to explain this phrase, I unpack it by providing the following terminological definitions:

- Positive – that which is deemed to be beneficial;
- Systemic – affecting all components of the economic system, that is, individuals and economic units, in a similar fashion all participants in transactions;
- Consistency – having the same directional effect, that is, benefits accrue at all levels but the degree of benefit will normally vary.

Such transactions embed mutual benefit instead of a stark zero-sum situation associated with the normal state of affairs of current policies that generate winners, losers and those who remain in a neutral policy impact state.

Reciprocal value-added

Positive systemic consistency relies on the ability of policy to bring about ***reciprocal value-added*** as a normal state of affairs in transactions in business-to-business, as well as in business-to-consumers, by changing ***zero-sum*** states of affairs into a ***win-win*** situation.

Thus, in a transaction, both the seller and the buyer gain an advantage. The seller gains a higher income by selling more than would be normal because of a more competitive price. The buyer is able to purchase a product or service at a comparatively lower competitive price.

How a Real Incomes Objective policy can deliver this type of benefit and reduce inflation is covered in Section 5. However, in the next Section 4, the nature of the economic performance failures listed on the previous pages will be assessed from the standpoint of these constitutional economic objectives.

This will point out the different mechanisms whereby the Bank of England monetary policy decisions on interest rates and government decisions on taxation have resulted in the failures indicated in the internal and external markets of the country.

4. Additional monetary mechanisms

Mechanisms?

In Part 1, I explained how increases in money volumes create a transition from rising asset prices becoming the source of cost-push inflation in the cases of land and real estate becoming higher priced or rental inputs for goods and services producers. This creates the incentive for anticipatory pricing to generalize cost-push inflation across the economy.

I also referred to the fact that it is this mechanism that causes money volumes to translate into rising prices in competing firms, and this is far from evident from an examination of the QTM or a key statement made by Milton Friedman.

However, monetary policy decisions have had a wide range of impacts as a result of additional mechanisms impacting economic units, individuals, and society in general.

The basic mechanism that converts asset price rises into a generalized cost-push inflation in goods and services, as described above, is just one example. The specific mechanisms contributing to other significant problems facing the UK economy and constituents are different, but each is related to erroneous monetary policy decisions based on the logic of the misleading QTM.

These problems include:

1. Income disparity and inequality
2. Increasing poverty

3. Corporate failures
3.1 Investment and productivity declines
3.2 Fall in the balance of payments
3.3 Reduced national production capacity and performance
4. Understanding wage settlements and unemployment (Phillips curve)
5. International monetary circumstances
6. Policy defects

In this section the mechanisms creating each of these six conditions are described.

1. Why income disparity rises

Asset holders and traders

The income levels of asset holders and traders benefit from rapidly rising asset prices such as land and real estate (property).
The volume of transactions and volume of money drives asset prices higher. Because of this effect, as money volumes rise, so do sales margins and income of traders.
In the meantime, the held assets accumulate in value, raising asset holder's wealth. The blue arrow in Figure 1 indicates the direction of price movements desired by asset holders and traders. A price rise from 1.00 to 2.00 doubles real incomes by moving from position A to point B.

Figure 1 Asset holder preference for movement of asset prices

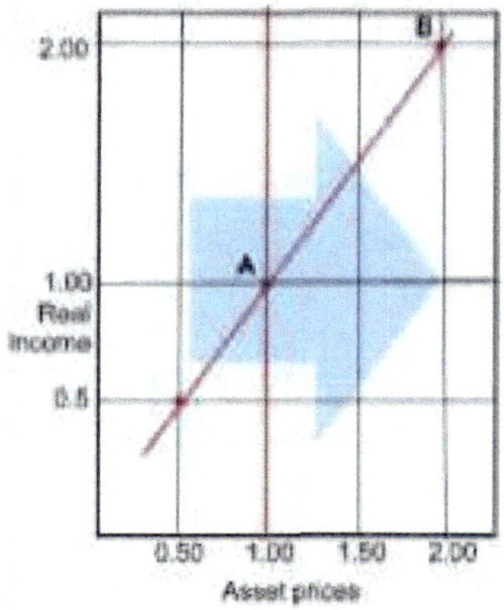

Wage-earners

In the case of wage-earners, nominal wages do not rise significantly from year to year. As shown in Figure 2, a doubling of goods and service prices will halve real incomes by moving the state of real income from A to B as a function of rising prices.

Figure 2 Wage-earner preference for goods and service prices

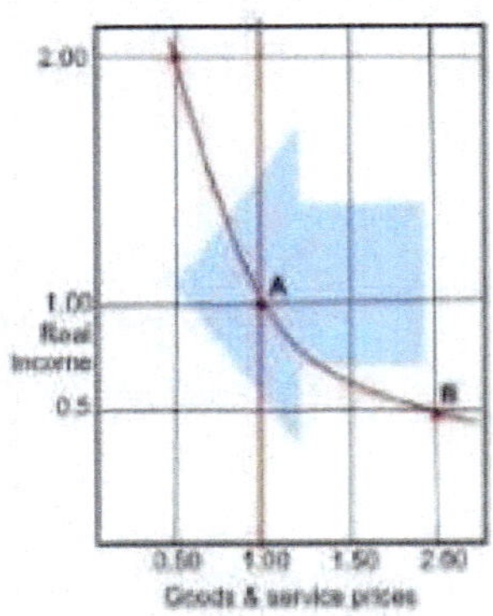

Therefore, the blue arrow indicates the preferred price movement by wage-earners. A short analysis shows all of these outcomes to be the result of the creation of zero-sum conditions which do not uphold the desired balance in the growth of real incomes or a positive systemic consistency able to support the interests of the state, society, economic units and individuals in a balanced fashion.

This is of particular significance in the understanding of why the Quantity Theory of Money is misleading and in identifying a policy to prevent these issues from arising.

As can be appreciated, asset holders' and traders' price movement preferences are diametrically opposed to wage-earner preferences.

The fact that in one case we refer to assets, and in the second case, goods and services, is not a matter of comparing apples and pears.

This is because the determinant of the real incomes of asset holders and traders are the very products they trade in or hold. As the prices of goods and services rise, real incomes decline.

Valuations

There is a long and well-established procedure used to evaluate the value of land and real estate where rises in its price is seldom referred to as inflation but, rather, as an increase in asset value regarded as positive and beneficial in terms of upward "valuation".

Constituent real income effect

Because prices of assets such as land and real estate (houses, offices, commercial and industrial units) are rising, there is a knock-on effect in housing markets and industrial and logistics units, causing a rise in rentals and prices. This raises business costs and the cost of living for families paying rent or attempting to purchase a home. This results in family and business costs rising and a corresponding rise in the prices of goods and services.

Once the inflation rate of goods and services begins to rise, the real demand begins to decline because the purchasing power of wages declines. This means that there will be difficulties faced by businesses and households to pay rent so that the return on rental properties will falter and the resales market will weaken resulting in such entities as hedge funds coming onto the scene and purchasing from middle income owners, usually at a discount.

When the United Kingdom modified its macroeconomic approach to place more emphasis on monetary policy in 1975, the average house price was £10,388 and the weekly average wage around £48. By 2023 the average price of a house was £258,115 and the average weekly wage around £600. Over that time period, wages increased by a factor of around 12.5 whereas house prices increased by a factor of around 25.

Therefore, house prices and rents as a component of the cost of living of average wages contributed to a halving of the purchasing power of wages for that component. At the same time, buying and selling houses and renting them remained profitable for those concerned.

Bank of England rhetoric

The Bank of England, while referring to "price stability" and also relying on the logic of the QTM, gives the impression that the price stability it refers to relates to goods and services. However, the objective of monetary policy decisions is to maintain the value of assets, because these also act as collateral for banks.

This is understandable.

Conclusion

The way in which monetary policy has been managed has contributed to a marked rise in income disparity between asset holders and traders and wage-earners, and the majority of those in the lower income segments.

The income disparity increase mechanism

In the case of income disparity this increased as a function of funds flowing into asset markets creating a particularly steep rise in prices that represent valuations of held assets as opposed to costs, resulting in the wealth and income of a small percentage of the constituency of the United Kingdom rising as a function of increases in money volumes. On the other hand, wage-earners facing rises in the prices of goods and services face a reduction in real incomes.

As can be appreciated this situation undermines any possibility of any prevalence of a positive systemic consistency.

2. Why poverty increases

The last section explained why asset holders and traders benefit from monetary policy decisions, while wage-earners do not.
The result of this differentiation is rising income disparity but also rising poverty.

What is poverty?

Poverty is a state of affairs where the income of someone in work is insufficient to purchase bare essentials.

Why this happens

An increasing number of British workers are ending up in this situation.

Whereas income disparity is the result of monetary policy augmenting the wealth of asset holders over wage-earners, poverty increases as a result of unadjusted wages combined with the rise of unit costs (cost-push inflation) reducing the accessibility of essentials to the lower income constituents.

To follow this graphically, we need to replace the conventional supply and demand graph which relates to the commonly presented Aggregate Supply and Demand (ASD) model with the Supply-Side ***Production, Accessibility and Consumption*** (PAC) model which provides more insights.

Aggregate Supply and Demand

As is self-evident, the aggregate supply and demand curve below, provides no information on the ranges of income and accessibility of prices to different categories of income.
The graph shows an assumed relationship between supply (line SS) showing supply rising with higher prices and demand (line DD) showing demand falling with higher prices, with the assumption that the market is cleared at the "equilibrium point "E" where supply is equal to demand.

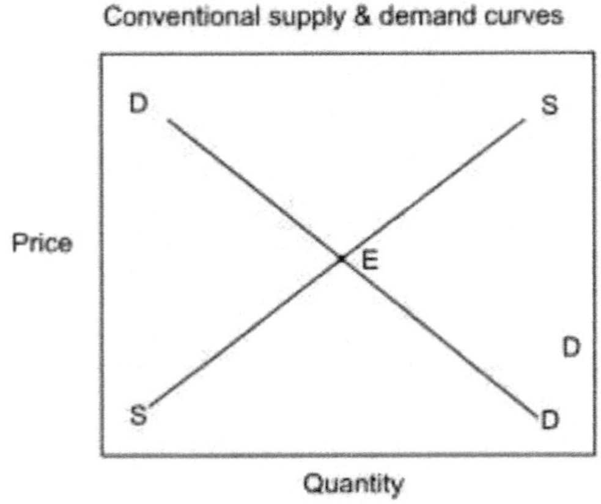

Production, Accessibility and Consumption

The Production, Accessibility and Consumption (PAC)[45] model provides a better insight into the distribution of product accessibility according to incomes and by making use of a "transactional envelope" which is a space demarcated by maximum feasible prices payable by a household or individual according to their disposable income and the average unit costs of production at a given scale of output.

Prices will be agreed somewhere between these two constraints depending upon total sales and the degree of competition.

The construction of this representation is shown in the diagrams below.

To construct the PAC graph shown at the bottom as Diagram 4, use is made of the distribution of disposable household incomes across the whole country as shown in Graph 1. This is inverted along the horizontal axis to place higher-income groups to the left as shown in Graph 2 so that income distribution runs from the bottom right to high on the left.

Graph 3 shows a plot across the disposable income range of the maximum feasible prices for a given product shown by

---

45 McNeill, H. W., "*Post-Covid-19, time to apply policies based on the Production Accessibility & Consumption Model (PACM) - Part 1 and Part 2*", Real Incomes.

the blue line associated with income levels and the unit costs of production at levels of market penetration from left to right in red.

This creates a *"transactional envelope"*.

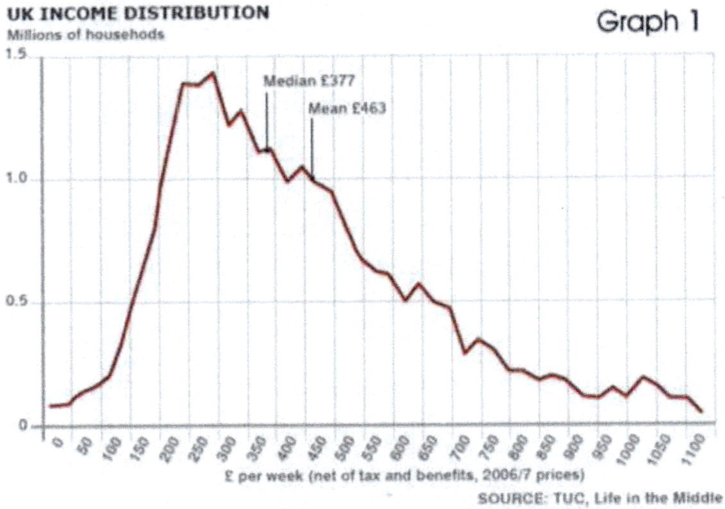

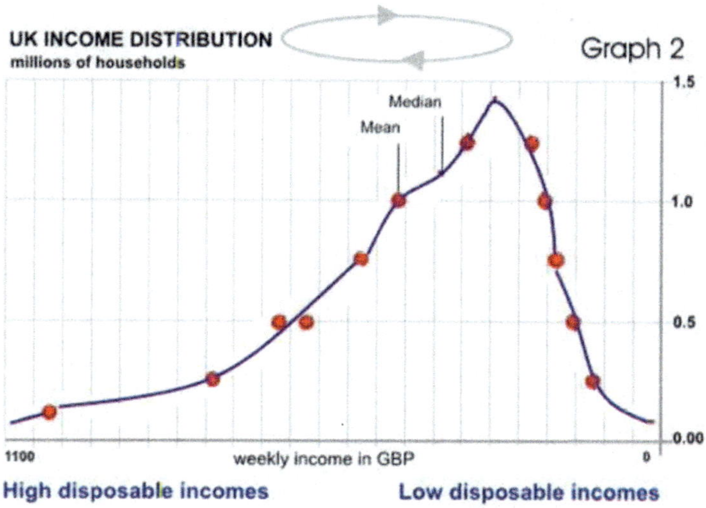
UK INCOME DISTRIBUTION
millions of households
Graph 2
1.5
Median
Mean
1.0
0.5
0.00
1100
weekly income in GBP
0
High disposable incomes
Low disposable incomes

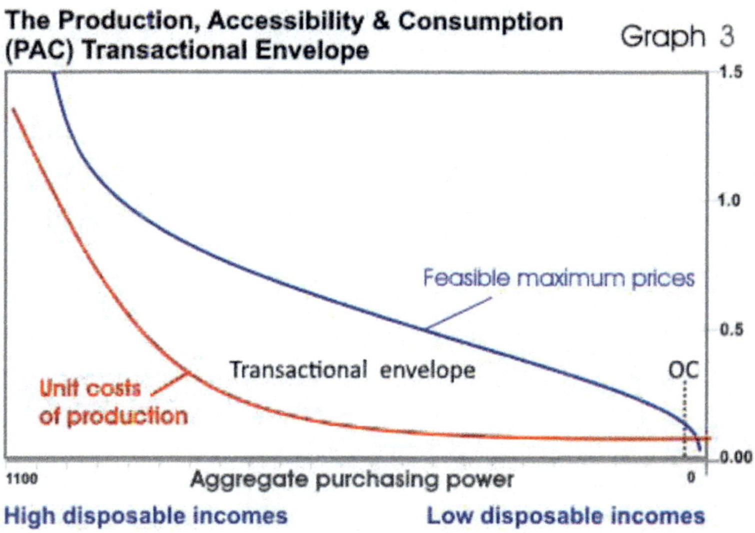
The Production, Accessibility & Consumption
(PAC) Transactional Envelope
Graph 3
1.5
1.0
Feasible maximum prices
0.5
Transactional envelope
OC
Unit costs
of production
0.00
1100
Aggregate purchasing power
0
High disposable incomes
Low disposable incomes

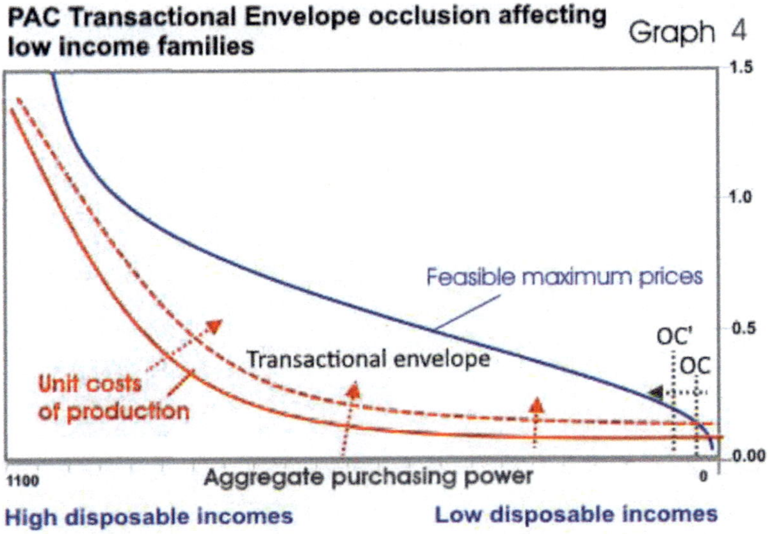

Thus, in Graph 3 the position 'oc' marks the point where everything to the right of that point is an ***occluded market*** and not accessible to those at that level of disposable income because their feasible price is too low for the supplier to make a profit.

Therefore, as cost-push inflation persists and unit costs (red line) rise, this causes the 'oc' position to move further left, meaning more people on low incomes will not be able to access the products at their feasible price.

Therefore, as a natural progression of cost-push inflation, poverty continues to rise.

Continued inflation results in lower income segments, where adjustments to wages tend not to keep up with an accumulating fall in the value of the currency and thereby disposable incomes fail to keep up with rising prices.

As a result, because monetary policy has never eliminated inflation, there is a growing income segment whose real incomes are falling on a constant basis.

During the last 50 years, employment has moved from skilled higher-paid industrial and manufacturing jobs to very low-paid service sector jobs. In 1975 38% of the working population worked in industry and manufacturing, in 2024 just 17% are employed in industry and manufacturing.

In 1975, 56% of the working population was employed in services and in 2024 it is 80%.

The services sector has amongst its lower-paid segments somewhat precarious employment conditions, including zero-hour contracts and an imposition of self-employment in the case of other services where all social overheads are on account of self-employed contractors.

In many cases fees are insufficient to cover such obligations.

Even in some companies, the accountancy regulations and corporate accounts for taxation classify labour as "costs", thereby tending to lower the priority of wage adjustments by slowing them down to increase current profits as a result of part of the function of anticipatory pricing.

Conclusion

Poverty is created by rising inflation combined with a failure to adjust low-income payment, often service sector employment, for the cumulative devaluation of disposable incomes caused by inflation.

This results in a constant decline in purchasing power and can finally lead to borderline cases of not being able to purchase basic essentials and having to resort to the use of food banks and other supports of various kinds.

The poverty creation mechanism

Lower income segments are often in jobs where there is weak bargaining power and absence of trade unions, such as in the case of so-called zero-hour contracts. In any case, consumer price indices (CPI) seldom represent the actual rise in prices of consumption "baskets" of lower income segments, resulting in inadequate upward adjustments even when there are wage adjustments.

As can be appreciated the desired state of a positive systemic consistency does not exist.

3. Why companies fail

Market dimensions

Rising costs reduce the area of the transactional envelope, which represents a fall in the dimensions of the market.

Throughput

As a result of declining consumption, company throughput falls, which increases the costs of overheads and fixed plant, raising costs.

This increases costs in what is already a cost-push state of operations of rising input costs.

The limits of anticipatory pricing

Whereas there is an initial feasibility to make use of anticipatory pricing to cover rising input inflation, the build-up of unit costs and the falling purchasing power of consumers also facing rising prices and declining real disposable incomes, results in volumes of sales peaking, followed by a trend towards a declining market size and depression.

Marginalization of companies as market shrinks

At any point in time, the number of operational companies and their capacities are linked to the previous market size associated with a higher turnover when companies made adequate margins.

With cost-push inflation, the degree of competition under such precarious circumstances rises. Therefore, the reduction in money volumes (M) increases the level of competition and as a result companies with higher costs, often smaller companies, find that their rate of return is too low to continue in business, and as a result different sectors begin to experience corporate failures.

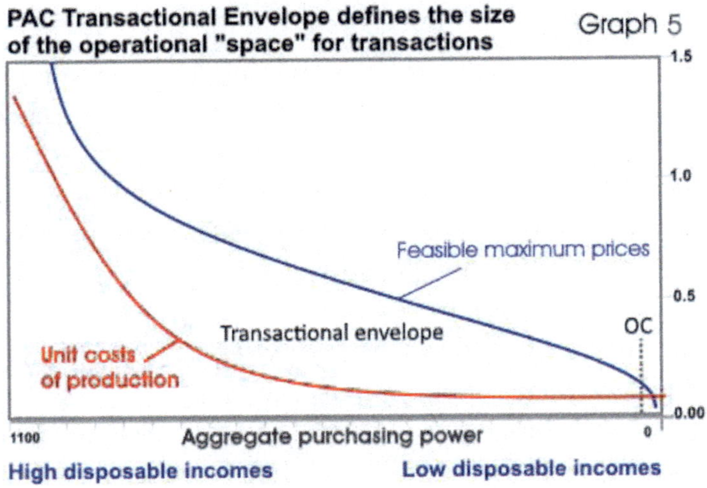

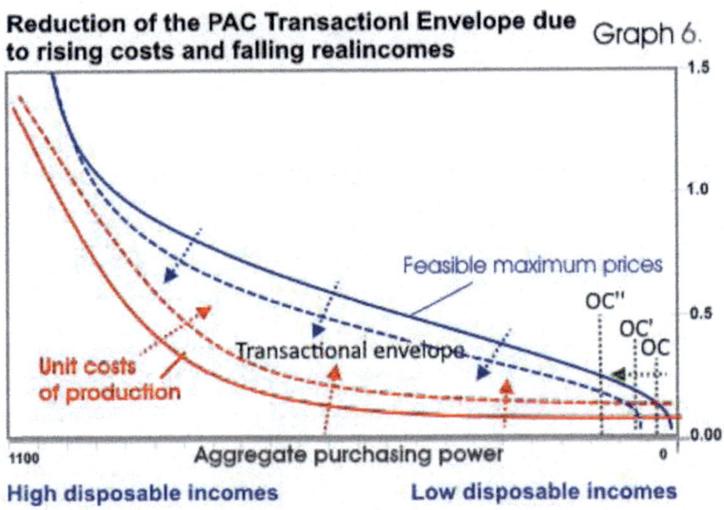

During QE, with most funds flowing into assets with a high rate of increase in prices, the volume of transactions in goods and services declines.

Banks dedicate more effort to lowering their risks by purchasing on their own accounts or lending out funds to corporations to buy assets.

With declining prospects for producers of goods and service providers, loans to these companies are perceived to be higher risk, resulting in higher interest rates and terms, such as the amount of collateral required.

This state of affairs exacerbates the impact of cost-push inflation.

Conclusion

The behaviour of banks implementing monetary policy decisions which incentivize asset purchase results in investment finance becoming more expensive because of a rise in perceived risk as goods and services companies lose turnover, leading to corporate failures and loss of jobs.

The desirable state of a positive systemic consistency is not upheld.

3.1. The corporate failure mechanism

Monetary policy decisions increase cost-push inflation and depress purchasing power and consumption, resulting in a reduction in the size of the market. Throughput reduction raises costs and, as a result of falling consumer purchasing power, the proportion of the population that can afford profitable prices declines, resulting in corporate failures.

Rates of corporate failure

In 2022 and 2023, the excess of corporate failures over corporate registrations which normally remain in balance was around 20,000 companies in each year. This is projected to reach 35,000 in 2024 resulting in a total of around 75,000 for 2022-2024.

3.2 Investment and productivity declines

Another very apparent transition over the last 50 years, which has been the actual cause of the deindustrialization of Britain, has been inadequate investment. As a result, rises in productivity have been too low to sustain a competitive industrial and manufacturing sector capable of competing with other countries undergoing an accelerating industrialization and growth.

Although those advocating offshore investment during the 1970s and 1980s did so to raise the profitability of their businesses, this impacted the productivity of onshore industry and manufacturing. A counter argument to criticism was that Britain's location in Europe could not compete on the basis of existing wages with offshore centres located largely in South East Asia.

However, Germany, with a similar resource cost structure to Britain, did not deindustrialize or lose manufacturing but rather invested to raise productivity to compete on the world stage and to develop the highest balance of payments for goods in the world. It was only in 2021 that China came close to achieving a balance of payments the size of that of Germany.

A notable characteristic of Germany's export success is that this rested not only on the output of large corporations including automobile production but also on the output of over 1,500 family firms and SMEs mainly in the advanced technology sectors.

One important underlying factor which assisted Germany to perform in this way was the fact that it requested lower-cost Russian gas to be piped to Germany under long-term contracts.

The issue of finance for investment

The question of finance for investment is of interest.

Nicholas Kaldor observed that bank loans for investment only accounted for a small amount of investments, with most funds coming from corporate cash flows.

A recent Bank of England assessment[46] of finance for SMEs agrees with Kaldor's assessment, showing that only around 20% of SMEs make use of bank loans for investment.

During the period 1975 through 2024 a considerable amount of investment flowed overseas representing lost funds to national investment.

---

[46] Bank of England, *"Identifying Barriers To Productive Investment and External Finance: a Survey of UK SMEs"*, Bulletin, 2024.

Overseas monetary flows are an important variable in the Value Theory of Money[47] whereas this does not feature in the Quantity Theory of Money.

3.3 Why the balance of payments in goods declined

Over the last 50 years, between 1975 and 2024, as increasing investment flowed to offshore production units, the proportion of the working population in industry and manufacturing in the UK declined from 38% to 17% of the working population.

This involved a loss in productivity and international competitivity of British output resulting in a fall in higher paid skilled jobs and a gradual decline in real incomes of wage-earners in contrast to the period 1945 to 1965.

During the same 50-year period, the services sector has expanded to employ 80% of the working population, mostly in lower paid jobs, whereas in 1975 it was around 56% of the working population.

Goods are produced by industry and manufacturing in activities involving design of products and of manufacturing processes. This innovative process is normally enhanced by the accumulation of human tacit knowledge[48] or practical competence in the conduct of repetitive tasks.

The design and management of operations uses explicit knowledge, including data on process performance and

---

[47] See: http://www.boolean.org.uk/library/Theories_of_Money.pdf

[48] See tacit knowledge in Annex 1

general awareness of cause-and-effect relationships across state-of-the-art technologies. These combine as a foundation for future innovation, leading to the improvement in efficiency and productivity embedded in products and devices used in all sectors of the economy and households.

However, with no industrial or manufacturing policy for the last 50 years and a reliance upon monetary policy decision cycles, funds have been flowing into overseas industrial and manufacturing investments.

Britain, as a result, has deindustrialized and lost higher paying jobs associated with industry and manufacturing. The failure to support industry and manufacturing has seen a loss of capabilities in the area of innovation because Britain is not making enough competitively priced goods, and the country has become too reliant on imports.

As a result, funds flow to those who innovate in other countries at the expense of potential innovators in Britain.

We now have the second most negative balance of payments in industrial and manufactured goods on the planet.

Conclusion

As a result of there having been no industrial or manufacturing policy and an over-reliance on monetary policy decision cycles over 50 years, and with no attention paid to the money drains represented, and specifically to the drain of an overseas flow of funds, a major decline in the balance of payments for goods occurred.

Corporate failures, falling investment and balance of payments reflects the absence of a positive systemic consistency.

4. Wage settlements and unemployment (the Phillips curve)

In 1958, Alban W. H. Phillips (1914-1975), published a paper entitled *The Relation Between Unemployment and the Rate of Change of Money Wage Rates in the United Kingdom, 1861-1957* [49] in which he set out the inverse relationship between money wage changes and unemployment in the British economy, based on the data set for that extensive period. The general relationship which came to be known as the Phillips curve is shown below as P-C.

It should be noted that the demand for higher wages is related to nominal incomes compared to changes in prices or income purchasing power. As price rises cause a fall in purchasing power of nominal wages, then pressure on wage demands rises. Therefore, there is a direct relationship between inflation, or the cost of living, and wage demands.

Note this is not related to unemployment.

---

[49] Phillips, A. W. H., "*The Relation Between Unemployment and the Rate of Change of Money Wage Rates in the United Kingdom, 18611957*", Economica, 1958.

The Phillips Curve

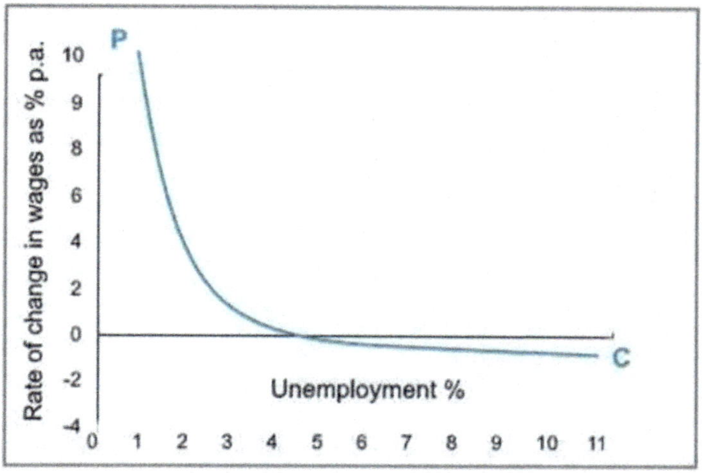

The PC line seems to reflect the relationship of

wage settlements not existing in isolation from general price inflation or falling real incomes..

Based on the Phillips curve, the impact of the petroleum price increases was unexpected because the coordinates of high inflation and rising unemployment moved off the P-C curve to a completely different location.

In the absence of adequate productivity gains, high unemployment resulting from high input cost-push inflation and absence of real increases in wages, resulted in rising unemployment while maintaining a high level of inflation.

Stagflation shifted the coordinates of the Phillips Curve to positions combining higher unemployment and inflation

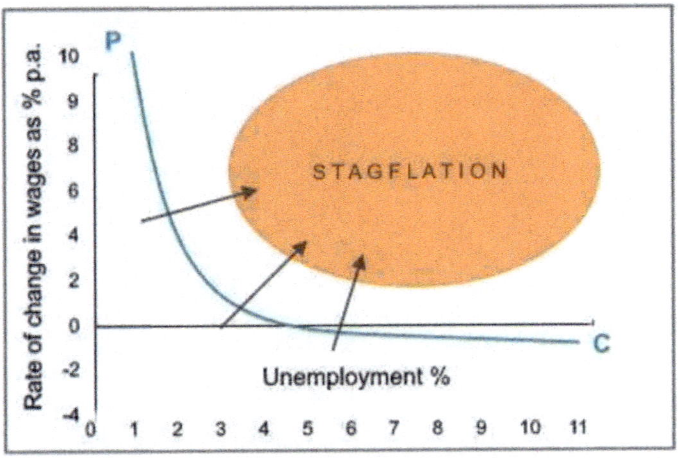

5. International monetary circumstances

Although a problem identified in the early 1970s, due to the significant rise in petroleum import prices imposed by OPEC, created a serious balance of payments imbalance, the medium to long-term state of the balance of payments always ends up as a function of productivity.

This is also the case for inflation and the exchange rate.

If productivity does not improve, the exchange rate of the pound against other currencies can fall, creating inflationary pressure arising from imports, and if no action is taken, the exchange rate of the pound against other currencies will continue to fall.

Currency wars

In the past, there have been what are termed currency wars whereby countries reduce their interest rates to lower their exchange rates to facilitate exports. If many countries attempt to use this approach to improve their balance of payments by raising exports, the situation is termed "currency war"[50].

Reverse currency wars

Reverse currency wars are a state of affairs where raising the value of a currency by attracting foreign investment by raising interest rates can create a differential in attracting foreign investment initially in other leading currencies such as the euro and the British pound.

Because the general productivity levels in the USA exceed those of the EU and UK, such behaviour restricts the ability of the ECB and the Bank of England to lower interest rates since these risk causing a decline in the exchange rate and investment in sterling.

Currency substitution wars

The United States dollar is the international reserve currency, and many trade activities have been dominated by markets in which quotations and transactions are completed using the dollar. Under the petrodollar regime, this was the case for international transactions in petroleum.

---

[50] Rickards, J., "*Currency Wars: The Making of the Next Global Crisis*", Portfolio, 2011.

Since the early 20th Century, the USA has made increasing use of financial sanctions as a tool in its foreign policy kit to wield influence over foreign countries.

In particular, of late, some 12,000 separate sanctions have been imposed upon the Russian Federation as part of USA and NATO retaliation against Russia for its military action against Ukraine. Of particular concern has been the sequestration of Russian foreign reserve assets to the tune of around $300 billion.

This has resulted in an increasing number of countries becoming concerned about falling victim to dollar-based coercion, imposed by the USA, to influence their domestic and trade policies.

There has therefore been a movement to attempt to substitute dollar-based transactions with the currencies of trading pairs, as well as to work out international payment settlement mechanisms for non-dollar-based transactions.
This movement is generally referred to as de-dollarization.

6. Policy defects

In the quest for a better theoretical and policy framework to safeguard real incomes, this short section summarizes the defects of conventional theory, giving rise to policy decisions that have been prejudicial.

The inappropriate nature of monetary policy instruments of interest rates and money volume control ignore the mechanisms that create cost-push inflation and therefore currency depreciation has been a constant factor over the last 50 years.

These instruments have had a generally prejudicial impact on the real incomes of the state, society, economic units, and individuals.

Monetary policy decision cycles have seen rising wealth and income in a small minority of asset holding and trading constituents and various levels of decline in real incomes across wage-earners.

The repetitive resort to austerity following inflationary periods is also associated with inadequate investment to raise productivity and has resulted in failing businesses and loss of employment.

Overall, monetary policy fails to achieve a state of positive systemic consistency.

Defects of supply-side economics

The other policy options outside the mandate of the Bank of England have included supply-side economics while releasing money through the lower marginal tax rates of higher earners. This marginal taxation initiative was not applied to companies, and there was no conditionality attached to the lower tax rate. As a result, there was no control over where those funds were used.

Naturally this meant that a good deal of the net of tax windfall was not allocated to investment but rather to personal and family expenditure resulting in a rise in income disparity. This also signified that the policy was unpredictable.

Its application in Britain was not successful.

Defects of tax allowances

Tax allowances and such things as "super-deductions" are not monitored or associated with any direct relationship or obligations to secure increased productivity or any impacts on unit prices.

Nothing in the Bank of England's monetary decisions helps improve the balance of payments for goods.

Keynesianism and supply-side economics have no specific reference to innovation and/or technical change.

The most notable characteristic of monetary and Keynesian theory and policy is the absence of any policy tools to incentivize innovation, changes in technology and technique, and rising productivity.

Above all, policy is not transparent, rendering policy decisions unpredictable in their impacts on the balance of payments, exchange rate, inflation and real incomes.

Policy requirements

In order to sustain real incomes, it is essential that policy gains control over the factors that create falling real incomes, such as terminating the use of inappropriate instruments such as interest rates, which exacerbate the decline in real incomes caused by cost-push inflation.

In the case of policies which release funds intended for investment to increase productivity, so as to enable reductions in unit prices of goods and services, it is essential that this is done in a way that ensures all such funds end up as investment to increase productivity and facilitate price moderation in an effective and predictable fashion.

There is a need for a "results-based" as opposed to an "expectations-based" policy so that, when marginal tax rates or other facilities increase funds for investment to lower prices, then such funds should only be released to beneficiaries when the price effects are actually put into effect or on the basis of delivered results.

Counter-inflationary policies need to have a short as opposed to a long-term impact to terminate the erosion in real incomes rapidly.

Business requires transparent rules to be able to take advantage of incentives in such a way as to result in profitable competitive operations. Such operations should provide a policy result of moderated or even reduced prices.

Above all, policy decisions need to be transparent and with predictable results in terms of improved balance of payments, exchange rates and inflation while avoiding austerity, signifying that the policy needs to have a substantive combined impact on productivity and real incomes.

5. Real incomes theory and policy

In this section, less reference will be made to conventional economic theory and policies but rather more to concepts and measures that are specific to the Real Incomes Approach to macroeconomics or RIO (Real Incomes Objective).

RIO is an approach to macroeconomic management that is an extension to constitutional economics, with the specific objective of managing the state of real incomes or purchasing power of the state, society, economic units and individuals.

This is an approach to economics underwritten by constitutional provisions of agreement on appropriate public goods in the form of indivisible laws and regulations established through public choice. This, by necessity, requires that economic policies be decided through a free participatory development process. The underlying principle is to define policies that are not arbitrary but consistent with enhancing the ability of economic units to adapt their performance to support agreed policy objectives on a compensatory basis.

Rather than base national GDP and growth rates measurement on nominal currency units, national income is based on the real incomes of the state, society, economic units and each individual.

Real incomes are the purchasing power of each constituent, and they need to be at least at a level which satisfies accessibility to essentials for each constituent.

The baseline objective of RIO economic policy is to at least maintain and normally increase the real incomes of constituents as members of workforces and as consumers.

Whereas policy does not establish real income levels in a declarative fashion, the policy instruments applied by RIO allow economic units and workforces, including the selfemployed, to manage their operations to be able to maximize their real incomes according to their specific orientation and the availability of resources to each individual or economic unit.

Each constituent and economic unit remains free to operate on the basis of unhindered decision-making and actions to pursue their objectives while being discouraged from hindering the pursuit of others in their objectives.

Price stability is not a policy objective since prices vary according to freely organized and executed transactions. However, RIO is structured to provide incentives for economic units and the self-employed to moderate or even reduce output prices while gaining adequate compensation.

However, as a general principle, RIO aims, via policy instruments, to move transactions from a common zero-sum nature to situations where enhanced productivity and efficiency result in transactions exhibiting mutual benefit to both participants in a transaction or a state of reciprocal value-added.

This upholds a state of ***positive systemic consistency,*** signifying a mutual and consistent benefit characterizing the transactions throughout the economy (system).

It is understood that each economic unit and constituents, as members of the workforce, also make up the majority of consumers, each of whom face unique circumstances in terms of real incomes and, in the case of economic units, face different conditions of cash flow, size of order book, technologies, costs of inputs, information on ways to increase productivity and ability to do so in terms of size of company, ability and experience of the workforce, ownership and management.

Because of this reality, it is not considered to be rational to impose arbitrary top down fixed policy instrument values in the form of taxation or interest rates, for example, because this will introduce differential impacts creating winners, losers and some who survive in a neutral policy impact state.

Because of this heterogeneity of real incomes status of economic units and constituents, RIO aims to support economic units and individuals as employed or self employed by providing the means to adjust their operations to maximize their real incomes while also augmenting the real incomes on those they are dealing with in transactions.

Rises in input prices (inflation) impact the purchasing power of producers of goods and services just as output prices (inflation) impact the purchasing power of consumers.

The measure of the balance of benefit transferred by companies can be estimated by the Price Performance Ratio (PPR) which is a measure of the efficiency with which input price changes are transformed into output price changes.

The Price Performance Ratio is the percentage response of unit output prices to a percentage change in Aggregate Unit Costs. It is a measure of productivity that estimates the real income impact by measuring the movement of output prices with respect to input costs.[51]

Thus PPR = dUP/dAUC

Where:

dUP is the percentage price response; dAUC is the percentage aggregate unit costs change.

Notice that this accommodated input inflation is from both exogenous (imported) as well as endogenous (domestic) sources.

Under the conventional policy framework, a common state is for companies to participate in anticipatory pricing.

The effect of this, in addition to the ongoing rises in costs associated with rises in asset prices or imported products

---

[51] What is presented here is the PPR for rising input costs inflation, but there are other versions for deflationary situations. These were introduced following the advice of Robin Matthews, Professor of Political Economy at Cambridge as feedback on a monograph I published on 3P in 1981. In a computer all possible cases can be handled by a Boolean decision tree.

such as energy resources, is to raise prices and prejudice consumer and workforce real income.

Given that anticipatory pricing is a common practice, under the Real Incomes framework, the objective is to apply the anticipatory pricing logic while providing incentives to encourage the most competitive but profitable economic unit responses to rising input prices.

However, rather than setting prices in a speculative manner and exacerbating the consumer real incomes status, the policy objective is to help economic units become more competitive by applying business rules to maximize the combination of sales and profits.

First of all, the only way a company can increase consumer real incomes is to lower the PPR to less than unity (<1.00).

A PPR of less than unity (<1.00) reduces inflation and raises the relative value [52] of the currency and real incomes of consumers.

On the other hand, company profits decline.

Income-price elasticity of demand (I-pEd)

The income-price elasticity of demand (I-pEd) measures the rise in consumption of a product or service associated with a relative fall in its price. Under inflationary conditions we are

---

[52] Relative value rises in comparison to the other cases of PPR equal to or greater than unity.

dealing with responses to falls in the rate of inflation or absolute fall in unit prices.

The "income-price" association recognises that the actual response to price falls depends upon the disposable income of the consumer and the price level. A fall in price usually results in more goods or services being consumed and therefore sold at the now lower relative unit price, signifying that a larger number of consumers will benefit from the incremental rise in real incomes.

The I-pEd is a very powerful factor in helping lower-priced products penetrate markets and it therefore levers the impact of marginal reductions in prices. The simple demand and supply notions of aggregate demand economics tends to ignore this important factor.

At the same time, although the margin per unit (profit) is lower, the aggregate profit over a larger number of units sold rises.

Economic recovery

Given the relative size of the UK's domestic market, compared with competing larger economies such as China, USA and Germany, it will be difficult for new industrial and manufacturing activities including all emerging technologies. It is evident that there will be a need for some form of financial support to ensure sufficient cash flow to expand and gain critical mass in terms of output.

Such support would include for example the technologies and products essential for a transition to sustainable existence under climate change (A Green New Deal).

As has been made evident, companies with PPRs of less than unity (<1.00) face lower profits. However, their price competitivity is moving in a competitive direction to both penetrate the market and to raise consumers' real incomes. Therefore, in order to maintain this benefit, RIO makes use of policy to raise the returns to companies who succeed in reducing prices or reducing the rate of price increases under cost-push inflationary conditions, by varying corporate taxation.

By changing the nature of corporate taxation to one that is levied according to the degree to which a company has reduced inflation, thereby created transactions that have a ***reciprocal value added***, it is possible to reduce inflation while augmenting the real incomes of both producers (profits) and the workforce as consumers (reduced cost of living).

The proposed policy designed to achieve this result is ***Price Performance Policy (3P).***

3P makes use of the PPR as a performance indicator and uses a simple policy instrument, the ***Price Performance Levy***, as a corporate tax to provide a positive incentive to companies to lower their PPRs to secure higher net-of-PPL profits.

The Price Performance Levy (PPL)

The most effective way to provide incentives is to allow the development of competitive advantage to be stimulated bottom up and on a profitable basis while securing rising productivity and expanding real growth and incomes at the national level.

This is the objective of varying corporate taxation or the Price Performance Levy (PPL) as a function of the PPR.

The principal objective of 3P is to assist companies to effectively reduce the rates of increase in inflation or applying absolute reductions in unit prices to gain PPL rebates and a higher net of PPL margin.

Companies not delivering on the inflation or unit price reduction objectives pay a higher PPL and end up with a lower net of PPL margin.

Price Performance Levy formulae

There are many ways to construct suitable PPL formulae depending upon objectives. Annex 3 provides more details on some options.

One basis for building a suitable PPL formula is to have a basic tax rate (B) of say 20% and an additional function related to the PPR that augments (surcharge) or reduces (rebate) the 20% according to the PPR value so as to vary the net of PPL margins received by companies. By way of example, the following formula is a "power" function for a PPL.

$$PPL = B.PPR^2$$

To see the operation of this PPL (PPL= $B.PPR^2$)[53], the table below shows the net margin obtained with different PPR scores.

As can be observed, the net margin rises substantially according to the movement of the PPR below unity (1.00)

Variation of net margins with PPR

Gross Margin	PPR	PPL	Rebate (-) Surcharge (+)	Net margin
100	1.20	28.80%	+8.80%	71.20
	1.00	20.00%	0.00%	80.00
	0.80	12.80%	- 7.20%	87.20
	0.60	7.20%	- 12.80%	92.80
	0.50	5.00%	- 15.00%	95.00

This is an effective way to provide an incentive by promoting the development of competitive advantage to be stimulated bottom up on a profitable basis and gained on the basis of rising productivity and expanding real growth and incomes at the national level.

[53] This formula is B multiplied by the PPR squared (raised to the power of 2).

The 3P policy mechanism makes use of existing market forces by allowing the income-price elasticity of consumption (demand) to create an acceleration in market penetration and growth in sales of goods and service dissemination of output from those companies who are successful in satisfying policy objectives by becoming more price competitive.

The associated effect is a dissemination of rising real incomes amongst consumers purchasing such output.

Business rules

Because 3P creates a profit maximization framework that accounts for the changing vertical costs profile due to input inflation and the options available to maximize profits associated with the income price elasticity of consumption, the procedures of price setting are not the same as marginal cost pricing.

Business rules provide guidance on the establishment of an operational rise in productivity as a basis for reducing unit costs as a reference for establishing the most advantageous competitive unit output prices by trading off price reductions against incremental sales volume increases and unit profits.

Marginal cost pricing is essentially a "***price-taker***" situation, whereas the RIO approach can only succeed effectively as a result of companies becoming competitive "***price-setters***". The reduction of risk thresholds associated with higher net of -PPL results is an additional direct incentive for companies to become "***price-setters***".

Therefore, in order to maximize profits under the 3P regime encouraging ***reciprocal value-added,***[54] there is a need for different business rules to guide corporate price setting tactics to maximize real incomes.

Appropriate business rules under 3P involve the following procedural steps:

- Observe and record the current prices in the market

- Measure the aggregate rise in unit costs, if any, over a projected period

- Review the feasible technical changes and substitution options to reduce unit costs

- Compare projections of cost trajectories for alternative technical packages[55] identified and based on capital-embodied and/or capital-disembodied [56] productivity, scale effects and the learning curve coefficient over a projected period
- Select a target price that increases the quantities sold at the end of the projected period based on the income-price elasticity of consumption (demand)[8]

---

[54] Reciprocal value-added where both sides in a transaction benefit from a raised real income effect

[55] Technical packages are alternative combinations of personnel, inputs and process technology

[56] Capital-embodied and capital-disembodied – see Annex 1.

- Calculate the associated PPR and PPL combination to maximize the net of PPL profit
- Calculate the most advantageous projected revenue resulting from increased sales (cash flow)
- Reiterate the previous 2 steps to arrive at an advantageous trade-off position between unit price and total sales revenue
- Apply the projected target price **NOW** and then operate to attain the target unit costs that justify that target price over the projected period

Points to note

First and foremost, establishing the right PPR is of fundamental importance because the PPR is in reality a measure of real productivity gain because it considers output prices which impact purchasing power and consumer real incomes (see Annex 1 on productivity).

The impacts of 3P

Immediate, as opposed to long-term impacts

3P accommodates cost push inflation either from imported (exogenous) or domestic (endogenous) sources.
The most notable benefit of 3P is that the impact on prices is immediate. So, the typical delay between interest rate changes and the onset of policy-imposed depression in real incomes is replaced by an immediate boost to real incomes. This is because anticipatory pricing has been changed to setting more competitive prices on a technical and costs control basis, so that applying business rules creates

immediate real incomes advantages for consumers and rise in sales for producers.

Under conventional investment projections, prices are usually adjusted only when unit costs are reduced towards the end of the investment cycle, which in some cases could extend beyond a year.

Under 3P this is replaced by ***price reductions at the beginning of the investment period*** and PPL rebates remain in place until the next price adjustment. This is designed to accelerate market penetration with more competitively priced goods and services and disseminates consumer benefits more rapidly.

The PPR estimates can only be calculated by establishing each new price at the beginning of each production cycle. The income-price elasticity of consumption effect with lower prices helps accelerate sales and throughput, which are drivers of the learning curve[57] costs reduction and build up of improving worker expertise and product quality enhancements.

Better assignment of investable funds

Unlike Supply-Side Economics (SSE), 3P directs tax rebates where they will have gained an advantage in lowering inflation as a result of investment.

---

[57] See Annex 1 Productivity

The 3P/PPL system only applies to companies while SSE is applied to high income earners and has no handle on where the tax windfalls would be spent; this is wasteful.

Default augmentation of real wages

Accepting that the majority of consumers are also members of the workforce, the 3P impact on the purchasing power of the pound and rise in the real incomes of consumers, by default, 3P also raises real wages of the workforce across the economy.

Production efficiency shaping demand

Aggregate national economic growth is a function of the contribution of each economic unit[58] to real incomes and the resulting status of workforce real incomes is the effective consumer potential consumption or demand, operating under price-moderated conditions.

Contributions to productivity

Different approaches to increasing productivity are summarized in Annex 1.

3P contributes directly to foster innovation and productivity as a sustained process that impacts real incomes directly.

Conventional productivity measures of output per hour, or full factor output, cannot provide a measure of the real

---

[58] Economic unit: An economic unit is a corporation, company, mutual, cooperative, specific public service function, or self-employed individual.

incomes impact because of lack of price information. This is the role of the PPR.

The real incomes multiplier

There are two forms of real incomes multiplier under 3P, which compound the impact of the PPR on repetitive transactions such as in association with money velocity (V) and the other is associated with sequential transactions in a supply chain (SC).

Money velocity real incomes multiplier

As is the case in all discussed money theories (QTM, Cambridge Equation and VTM)[59] there is a variable (V) representing the "velocity of circulation of money" as the number of repetitive transactions associated with a specific quantity of money (M). See online document, "Theories of Money"[60].

Depending upon the average PPRs associated with transactions, if the velocity rises above unity (V=1.00), then the impact of the PPR will rise, resulting in a fall in the rate of inflation or an absolute price fall.

This is shown in the two tables below. One is for the rising input inflation case (dynamic) and the other for stable input costs (static) making possible absolute unit price reductions.

---

[59] See: http://www.boolean.org.uk/library/Theories _of_Money.pdf

[60] http://www.boolean.org.uk/library/Theories_of_money.pdf

Real Incomes multiplier effect associated with the velocity of money with a 10% inflation input (dynamic) on consumer level of inflation and real incomes

inflation Input	Average PPR	Money Velocity	Cumulative PPR	Final Price Inflation
10%	0.80	1	0.80	8.00%
		2	0.64	6.40%
		3	0.51	5.10%
		4	0.41	4.10%

Real Incomes multiplier effect associated with the velocity of money with a 10% inflation input (static) on consumer level of inflation and real incomes

inflation Input	Average PPR	Money Velocity	Cumulative PPR	Final Price Inflation
10%	0.80	1	0.80	80
		2	0.64	64
		3	0.51	51
		4	0.41	41

Supply chain real income multiplier effect

In a policy framework where the PPR is used as a measure of price performance related to inflation, there is a real incomes multiplier effect measured as the net reduction in inflation associated with sequential transactions in a supply chain.

This becomes effective if companies have a PPR of less than unity as a real income multiplier effect. The more companies within a supply chain, the greater will be the inflation reduction impact over the whole supply chain.

For example, assuming each company within a supply chain has an average PPR of 0.80, the two tables below show the effects of increasing numbers of SC participants (nodes) on inflation in a dynamic and static case.

Supply real incomes multiplier effect associated with the number of supply chain (SC) operatives (nodes) on a 10% inflation input (dynamic) on consumer level inflation and real incomes

inflation Input	Average PPR	Number of SC nodes	Cumulative PPR	Final Price Inflation
10%	0.80	1	0.80	8.0%
		2	0.64	6.4%
		3	0.51	5.1%
		4	0.41	4.1%

Supply real incomes multiplier effect associated with the number of supply chain (SC) operatives (nodes) on a 10% inflation input (static) on consumer level inflation and real incomes

inflation Input	Average PPR	Number of SC nodes	Cumulative PPR	Final Price Inflation
10%	0.80	1	0.80	80
		2	0.64	64
		3	0.51	51
		4	0.41	41

Assets as a specific class of goods

Just as 3P can reduce the rate of increase in prices of goods and service company outputs as well as bring about absolute price reductions, so, applying this policy to assets[61], as a specific class of goods can help slow down asset valuations and price rises. This has the advantage of reducing the impact of those assets that are used as inputs to goods and services production companies or to households in the form of house prices and rents.

This effect, which impacts asset sales by applying PPLs, might be implemented by applying different PPL formulae according to the desired regulatory requirements, decided on the basis of public choice related to the basic levy B.

The effect would be somewhat like a capital gains tax. The PPR determination could apply in the context of considering "improvements", especially in the case of land and buildings. These costs would enter as AUC (Aggregate Unit Costs) in the PPR formula, thereby lowering the PPR.

It would seem that an appropriate adjustment would also be useful to distinguish between private owner-occupied housing so as to apply a lighter or zero PPL regime, while commercial assets would be subject to a tighter inflationary (valuation) control.

From rentier to productive activities

Raising the returns on productive activities and moderating returns on assets is likely to change the concentration of investment as a move from asset-based rentier activities to a

---

[61] Land, real estate (buildings), commodity positions, precious metals, rare objects and art, shares, financial instruments, cryptocurrencies.

growth in real productive activities under a lower risk 3P environment.

Therefore, a considerable amount of financial resources associated with asset holdings might be released in the form of equity investment in the production of goods and services within the more competitive lower investment risk 3P regime.

Debt reduction

The shift in investment to real productive activities under 3P will result in higher cash flows and a reduction in the need to rely on external interest-bearing debt.

This would result in investments costing less under the 3P environment, providing a boost to investment and productivity under a 3P regime.

The role of savings banks

One of the general criticisms of the British banking environment is the dominance of just five large banks and where only about 20% of SMEs use their services for investment.

Suggestions have been made[62] that Britain needs a large number of localised savings banks to support SMEs similar to the German model and also a model adopted by China.

---

62 Mkhaiber, A., & Werner R. A., "The relationship between bank size and the propensity to lend to small firms: New empirical evidence from a large sample", Journal of International Money and Finance 110 (2021) 102291

Such banks have more interest in assisting their local clients, whereas large banks' main interest is in having sufficient collateral to cover possible losses.

However, 3P has a specific role of augmenting SME cash flow and to reduce the need for the additional costs associated with loans for investment. It is hoped that the acceleration of growth in scale resulting from market penetration should attract equity investment as opposed to loans.

Industries with varying annual output

A production sector subjected to annual variations in costs is agriculture, where yields can vary from year to year as a function of the weather.

These variations impose significant variations in unit costs because the same input total will be associated with high or low harvests.

Agriculture is therefore an ideal candidate for 3P because farmers can avoid significant losses in bad years and remain in business because there is an automatic adjustment made for high cost years depending upon sales prices which remain a decision to be made by famers.

Public services

Public services in delivering goods and services can be managed under 3P with ease.

However, since there is in reality no internal market involving transactional prices but rather an association of cost centres, the performance of activities would be based on shadow-PPRs or comparisons of projected unit cost attainments, based on PPR estimates or based on the use of an embedded nominal fixed margin.

Shadow pricing

This creates a shadow price associated with a specific unit cost. This concept is explained in Annex 4.

Application in public services

3P, on this basis, can be applied to care services, the National Health Service, NHS human capital, general practitioners, elderly care, National Institute for Health & Care Excellence, generics, general preventative procedures, etc.

Private public service goods and service providers

All private suppliers to public services operating under 3P could operate under very price-competitive conditions by contributing to service productivity by reducing costs under the 3P regime..

Application to utilities

Large-scale operations such as utilities including energy, communications, water and rail transport are ideal candidates for 3P administration because of the well understood operational structures based on networks and technologies simplifying the administration information management systems.

Devolved governments

One of the notable issues in the devolved governments of Scotland, Wales and Northern Ireland is the limited or no right to rise taxation. Since 3P does not in essence raise taxation but rather could manage financial resources to increase real growth and real incomes in a devolved manner it would seem that 3P is a suitable vehicle for the promotion of a more participatory and shared effort in economic recovery, including all countries in the United Kingdom.

Relationships between productivity (PPR) and the Phillips curve under 3P

It is arguable that by raising productivity to sufficiently high rates and applying these gains to lowering output inflation, the rises in wage rates associated with low unemployment would be lower because the purchasing power of the currency would be higher and therefore the motivation for demanding higher rates of wage rises would be less.

In many cases where the purchasing power of the pound is rising, it is likely that there would not be any necessity for wage increases.

In schematic form, the original Phillips curve is used to set out different productivity and pricing curves in the diagram on the next page.

Low productivity with high PPRs would be likely to produce high wage rises with low unemployment. This is the original a'-a curve.

A higher level of productivity combined with a lower PPR is likely to result in a lower rate of wage rises with low unemployment, as shown by the curve b'-b.

The objective of 3P is to encourage a combination of higher productivity with low PPRs and a curve approximating c'c so as to contain the levels of inflation at low unemployment.

Notional positions of Phillips Curve with different levels of productivity from a low, b median and c high productivity

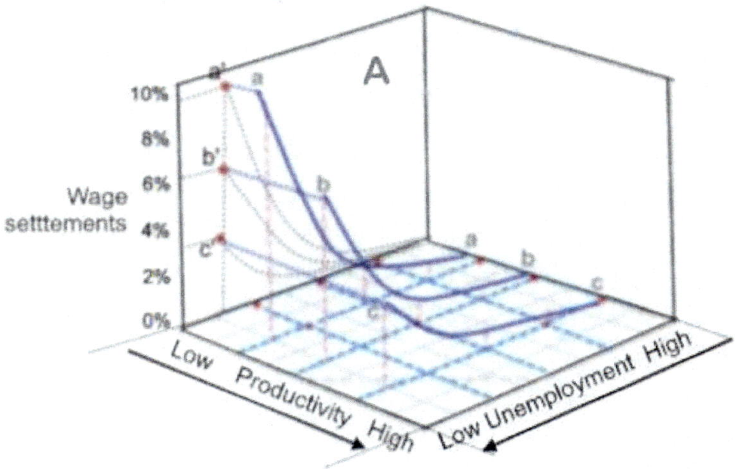

By bringing inflation down to lower levels, there is an enhanced probability of these levels of inflation being absorbed by the next phase increases in productivity. This compound graph can be projected in a 3D representation, showing the relationship between inflation, productivity and unemployment. Where productivity is able to lower inflation, the aim of Real Incomes Policy is to trade off ***price***

productivity against ***physical productivity***, which [63] is essential to secure unit ***costs control***.

The degrees to which this trade-off can be effective depends upon process technologies and the techniques that labour forces have learned to deploy. The backplane on the left of the 3D graph labelled A is shown below to show the impact of raised productivity on the position of the original Phillips curve.

Phillips Curve position with different levels of productivity
a' low through c' high

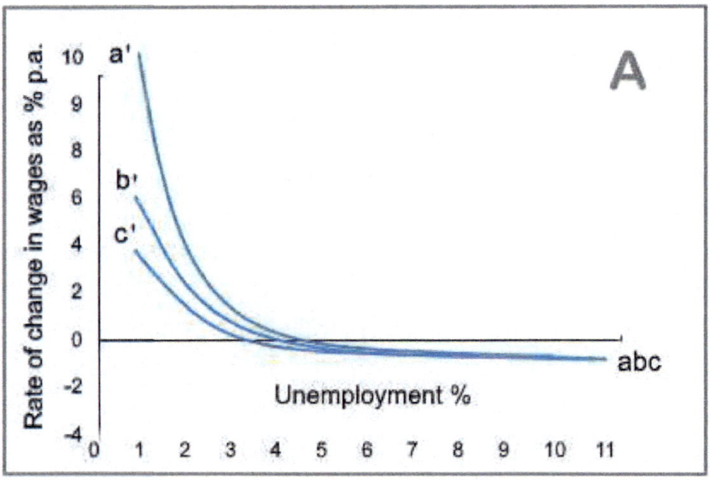

[63] To explore the distinctions between price productivity and physical productivity, see Annex 1 *"Productivity"*.

Thus, lower PPRs result in the motivation for higher wage settlements declining because real wages are higher under the 3P regime.

Because of the mixed reality of combinations of productivity, types of sectors, international markets and trade it is likely that the Phillips Curves for the period 1975 through 2024 have no relationship to the period Phillips analysed 1861-1957.

The overall combination or per company policy response to 3P and the real incomes multiplier effect results in a generalized support or rise in real incomes where specific technologies, such as information and communications technologies, enable trends in absolutely lower unit prices.

As a result, this benefit is enjoyed by consumers, most of whom make up the workforce.

This gain in productivity should lower the levels of any settlements on wages that have fallen behind in the timing of any necessary increases in nominal wages.

Although the current assumption is that as unemployment falls, all wage settlements become higher, it is apparent that this effect would be reduced to lower settlements if the productivity of the economy measured, in terms of a lower PPR, was higher.

Price Performance Policy and public choice

As described by James Buchanan, constitutional economics [64] includes the process of a common identification and agreement on a moral form of behaviour to support the interests of the state, society and the individual, arrived at through public choice.

There are two aspects of public choice operations under such a framework.

1. Like proposals for variations in taxation, 3P can be a proposal in which the electorate can express preferences according to the basic tax rate of the Price Performance Levy (B) and any associated wage payment procedures (see below). These can be related to industry and manufacturing technology types.

2. Unlike conventional taxation and interest rates, 3P allows companies to alter their PPR values so as to set their Price Performance Levy obligations to feasible rates. This provides management with increased degrees of freedom to lower the operational risks associated with investment and profitable innovation[65].

Therefore, although basic tax rate can remain an item of democratic public choice and is established as a top-down administered imposed value, the incidence of that tax rate is in reality set according to an optimization process adapted to

---

[64] McNeill, H. W, "*The importance of Constitutional Economics*", Real Incomes Approach, 2012

[65] Not all innovations turn out to be profitable

the specific conditions of each company as a bottom-up operation enabling fine-tuning of marketing strategies.

In terms of constitutional economics, this represents an adjusted concept of "public choice" what is being decided in terms of corporate operations remaining with economic unit management and workforces.

Public and group choice

Within the confines of laws and regulations designed to prevent the pursuit of interest of individuals or groups constraining the pursuit of interest of other individuals and groups, there is a further effect of an improving distribution of incomes by creating an uplift for all real income levels as a result of the reduction or elimination of inflation to reduce income disparity and the incidence of poverty.

Mutuals, cooperatives and wages

In the case of mutuals and cooperatives PPL rebates and surcharges applying to profits, could be applied to shareholder dividends and workforce incomes (wages).

Thus, mutual and cooperative organizations that do not have external shareholders can often gain from a vertical costs structure that is around 11% lower than public limited companies with external shareholders because the shareholders are the workforce.

The alignment of workforce incomes with corporate pricing decisions is likely to encourage less risky behaviour but at the same time offer rewards to these groups who wish to maintain growth in corporate market share and growth in real incomes. This provides an underlying incentive for group pricing decisions that both stimulate real growth and sustain employment.

Quantitative monetary considerations and the future of money markets

The Value Theory of Money[66] identified some of the main missing variables in the Quantity Theory of Money, and 3P is designed to eliminate their impacts on inflation and the value of the currency.

On the other hand, 3P also facilitates the growth in cash flows, use of own equity as opposed to bank loans and this can help reduce SME debt.

However, consideration of the quantity of money in circulation remains an unavoidable issue under the Real Incomes Approach and a macroeconomic policy framework such as 3P.

The underlying incentive of 3P is an emphasis on a sustained rise in productivity and a rise in the purchasing power of the pound. This is made possible by moderated price setting, the relationship between the PPR and PPL, and the net of tax status, which remains under the control of management and workforces.

The 3P objective is not only to lower the risk of investment but also to accelerate the rate at which productivity rises, and market share is gained by companies that are more responsive to 3P incentives.

---

[66] See http://www.boolean.org.uk/library/Theories_of_Money.pdf

In summary, 3P can be expected to achieve:

- Higher corporate growth rates in terms of the mix of volumes of sales and margins
- Stable or rising currency purchasing power
- Rising real wages either as a result of currency purchasing power or wage levels linked to agreements linked to corporate performance
- Rising consumption and demand under conditions of more efficient, more-for-less (MFL) production
- MFL production is a critical requirement to ensure environmental carrying capacity and preservation
- Declining poverty in the lower income segment ranks;
- Because there is a combination of raised productivity and moderated falling prices, the majority of growth will be real growth.
- Rising balance of payments in goods
- Rising import substitution
- Falling income disparity
- Falling poverty
- More transparent policy
- More predictable policy decision outcomes

Monetarism on the brink

The principle preoccupations of monetary policy have, on the one hand, been to defend the balance of payments and the exchange rate and to lower inflation to an arbitrary target of around 2%, which still erodes real incomes.

The balance of payments, inflation and the resulting exchange rate are all functions of productivity and the range of competitive goods and services that are available in the United Kingdom in exchange for sterling.

While not making gold equivalent to productivity, it is self-evident that the purchasing power of the pound and confidence in the currency as an asset as well as a means of exchange and accounting, rest with the levels of productivity and competitivity across all sectors reflected in the balance of payments and exchange rate.

It is therefore also evident that, far from being related to output, money volumes need to be related to an appropriate measure of productivity to consider the transition in rates of price movements between input and unit output prices.

The best measure of this price productivity is the Price Performance Ratio (PPR) which is a key variable in the Value Theory of Money.

A problem with international development projects

Even under the strictest project investment evaluation frameworks, such as those imposed in international development banks and agencies lending, the "investment in a promise" prevails where projects are designed and evaluated and subjected to technical and estimated economic rates of return (ERR) analyses, including cost benefit analysis (CBA).

In 1992, an internal review[67] of the World Bank project portfolio found that 35% of projects failed, and in infrastructural and agricultural projects, the rate of failure approached 45%. It was also noted that, despite internal regulations requiring that all funded projects be subjected to CBA before being presented to the Board, only around 25% of funded projects had CBA assessments.

Projecting this across all private and international agency project investments of around $215 billion per year, this is equivalent to a loss of $75 billion[68].

The inflationary problem had the effect of causing longer term projects' funding base to eventually lose purchasing power, leading to multiple reschedules, overruns and eventual cancellations.

While I was the Environmental Economist for the G7 Brazilian Rain Forest Trust Fund at the World Bank this was an important topic of concern amongst staff and there were active NGO campaigns[69] and considerable media coverage criticising the Bank with an emphasis on the poor performance of environmental and natural resources projects as being amongst the worst performers.

The Bank promised reform.

---

67 Wapenhans W., "*The Performance of the World Bank Project Portfoilo*", Portfolio Management Task Force, 1992.

68 OQSI-Open Quality Standards Initiative report 2020

69 Rich, B., "*Foreclosing the Future*" Island Press, 2013.

18 years later, in 2010, the Independent Evaluation Group of the World Bank conducted a review[70] of the role of CBA in World Bank projects to find that over 75% of Board approved and fully funded projects still had not been subject to CBA, and failure rates remained of the same order as that reported in 1992.

Under a 3P regime, such waste can be avoided[71].

The 3P macroeconomic framework is supportive of international economic development

The 3P environment provides a way to increase returns and lower the risk of investments for project and corporate adjustments and technical change to lower unit costs to achieve more competitive and accessible pricing.

Besides developed economies, such a capability is an urgent need in transition and low-income developing countries.

The counter-inflationary impact of a 3P macroeconomics regime can radically improve the performance of economic development projects, contributing to world efforts in combatting climate change and environmental degradation.

---

70 Independent Evaluation Group, "*Cost Benefit Analysis in World Bank Projects*", World Bank, 2010.

71 McNeill, H. W., "*The impact of trends in the international development environment on project performance*", Series: Decision Analysis, Series: Decision Analysis, Development Intelligence, London, 2020.

In this way, the advance of project financial tranches can be brought under more objective control. The 3P tendency to eliminate inflation and build up cash flow is also an important contribution to preventing projects over-running phase budget estimates, encountering increasing debt and risking cancellation.

Increasing, productivity generates faster project payback and reduces debt, and ongoing operations become less reliant on debt and increasingly able to become sustainable using cash flow to feed incremental investments.

Concluding

This discussion has set out arguments for the emergence of a new front to constitutional economics, which combines with elements a better use of money/savings with a view to promoting productivity and innovation as the motors for real economic growth and development.

The new front to constitutional economics is that aspects of monetary policy are transferred to the fiscal regime where constituents can be offered the public choice of basic corporate tax rates (B) where these can be related to wage payments.

The nature of 3P is that the corporate taxation regime provides for an adaptability of the tax regime to individual corporate conditions through group choice, with the option of including wage bonuses related to the Price Performance Levy rebates.

There is, therefore, a devolution of considerable degrees of freedom for companies to exercise optimization of growth and profitability and at a lower risk as a result of distinct business rules involving the combination of unit margins and a more effective market penetration and increased sales.

The 3P system, by only providing incentive benefits to performing companies, eliminates to a significant degree Ludwig von Mises' "*calculation and knowledge problem*"[72] associated with attempting to centralise inflation control with regard to interest rates and money volume issuance, can help transition the economy towards higher rates of investment from cash flow and savings by increasing the returns on equity in a low inflation environment.

The ultimate objective of sustaining high rates of productivity and innovation as the drivers of economic growth has a counter-inflationary objective that cannot be achieved on the basis of conventional monetary policy decisions based on the orientation of the Quantity Theory of Money (QTM).

The Value Theory of Money [73] provides an alternative foundation for explaining the impacts of the main determinants of the quantity of money in the goods and services domain as well as unit prices in a more precise manner than the QTM.

---

[72] McNeill, H. W., "*Ludwig von Mises' calculation and knowledge problem revisited*", Real Incomes Approach, an assessment of von Mises' *1920, "Economic Calculation in the Socialist Commonwealth"*

[73] http://www.boolean.org.uk/library/Theories_of_Money.pdf

The analysis of the contribution of the VTM variables to inflation, including the counter-inflationary impact of 3P related productivity, provides a more complete picture of both the theory and practical proposition of 3P as an effective alternative to monetarism while establishing productivity as an essential element of real growth.

Conclusions so far

Critical factors

Monetary policy has proven incapable of eliminating inflation and therefore has been unable to avoid depressing the purchasing power of the pound and real incomes.

Even the stated policy target for "price stability" as an inflation rate of 2% represents a continuation of real incomes depreciation equivalent to -18% each decade.

Over the last 50 years, this policy "target" has represented an overall depreciation of purchasing power of 63.6% and the average inflation rate over the same period was 5%, signifying a total depreciation in purchasing power of in excess of 92.7%.

As is evident, monetary policy has not been effective in eliminating inflation or in meeting the target of "price stability".

Income disparity resulting in poverty can only be resolved by implementing policies that result in companies raising their productivity in terms of more-from-less so as to be able to pay higher wages and moderate or reduce prices to control inflation thereby raising real incomes in general.

Substituting financial leverage risk with productivity accumulation and internal finance

As a result, there is a short-term reduction in the rate of inflation or absolute price reductions associated with a sustained medium or longer-term rise in productivity.

The procedure can be repeated as the new unit cost level is attained to initiate another learning curve trajectory associated with a further reduction in inflation or absolute price levels.

This approach involves no public funds; it substitutes the riskier option of financial loan-based investment and leverage leading to lower-risk self-funded phases dedicated to the build-up of productivity over the medium to longer term.

As a result, under the 3P environment, anticipatory pricing is transformed into predictive pricing and sales volumes associated with desired margins or profits.

3P effects a more positive control over inflation in comparison with the vagaries of interest rate setting or taxation avoiding the prejudice inflicted upon constituents and economic units..

3P is in essence a non-monetary inflation control policy.

3P can help establish a generalised positive systemic consistency throughout the economy as a positive contribution to levelling up across the countries of the United Kingdom.

6. RIO is a new macroeconomic supply side paradigm

This short section is to call attention to why RIO is a completely new macroeconomic paradigm that draws nothing from Keynesian variants, monetarism or what was referred to as supply side economics.

Starting out in 1975 I began work on the development of a way to defeat stagflation without any pre-established notions of where that would lead me but by mid-1976 I realised that the most important indicator was real incomes.

Robert Mundell was also working on a solution to stagflation but he began this quest at a slightly earlier date.

We both came up with different approaches to a supply side solution. Mundell's version became known as "Supple Side Economics" (SSE) which involved lower marginal tax rates for high income earners. The very early explanations of SSE were that this would result in more funds being invested in the hope of raising productivity and lowering unit costs and prices of goods and services.

When this was attempted in the United Kingdom it led to over 600,000 families losing their homes to repossession as a direct result of monetary policy which also raised interest rates to a high level.

The reality is that SSE had no control over how tax windfalls would be spent and in both the UK or USA and the result was a significant rise in income disparity, a significant rise in government deficits and a reduction in budgets assigned to social programmes. In addition, there was a rise in unemployment. There was a fall in inflation but this was more related to an imposed depression and falling energy prices.

My own proposed solution is also supply side but quite distinct from Mundell's SSE, Keynesian variants and monetarism, all of which support an aggregate demand or money volume approach.

As I observed as a student as far back as 1964, unit prices of goods and services are set directly by companies independently and free from arbitrary interference arising from Bank of England monetary policy decisions, changes in interest rates or arbitrary centrally imposed set rates of taxation.

Since "Supply side" refers to companies that produce goods and services so it should be self-evident that trying to influence their performance by providing high income earners with higher net of tax incomes has very little relevance to corporate productivity other than raising aggregate demand creating a productivity neutral growth measured solely in terms of amount of money in transactions.

The normal understanding of Keynesian and monetary logic is that more funds in the economy as aggregate demand (Keynesian) or money volume (monetarism) will result in increased demand and economic growth. What is notable is that neither of these policy approaches have any influence on productivity but simply see demand as a means of increasing levels of acquisition of the available range of goods and services.

There are, however, two far more powerful factors that can generate higher and sustained real growth:

1. One is ***productivity*** in its contribution to the lowering of unit costs opening up options to lower unit prices.

2. The other is the ***income-price elasticity of demand*** for each good or service which drives the distribution of more competitively priced goods and services through the economy increasingly as unit prices fall.

This powerful combination results in a rise in purchasing power of disposable incomes and a rise in real incomes throughout the economy and real growth.

Simply raising aggregate demand or applying lower marginal tax rates doesn't alter productivity and has no control over price rises due to inflation. As a result, the full power of income-elasticity of demand is ignored in the Keynesian, monetarist and SSE approaches.

RIO's macroeconomic proposition, Price Performance Policy (3P) applies a conditional lower marginal taxation rate to companies and not to high income earners. Companies can enjoy lower corporate taxation according to their unit price responses to input prices and the degree to which rises in productivity and lowering of unit costs enables companies to lower inflation. This of course benefits all consumers and the workforce by raising their real incomes. Such reductions in unit prices are a direct result of enhanced productivity on a profitable basis. This is incentivized by a corporate taxation (PPL) that varies with the corporate unit price response to aggregate unit input costs (PPR).

Nevit Turk has described 3P, unlike all other policies, as a "transactional macroeconomic policy"[74] being responsive to

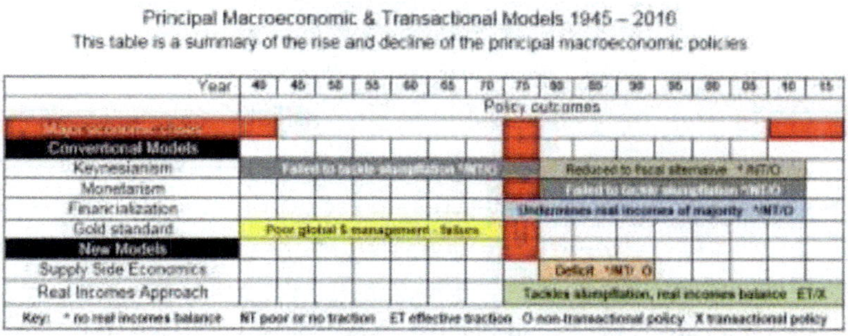

corporate conditions.

He included a comparative table which can also be found on the Real Incomes website where there is a 2015 map of comparisons between Keynesian, monetarism and 3P policies[75].

---

[74] Turk, N., *"Price Performance Policy - the last policy standing Why not give it a try?"* Agence Presse Européene, 2015

[75] McNeill, H. W., "Synthesis", Real Incomes, 2015.

The Bank of England's Bulletin has reported that SMEs generally avoid bank loans to invest and only about 20% use banks for this purpose. 3P helps build up company cash flow rendering them less dependent on external loans being able to invest from cash flow at a lower cost. This is an important advantage for SMEs who find conditions of loans from British banks to be onerous and risk prone.

As a result, 3P as a different and innovative fiscal scheme can control inflation and stimulate real growth at the same time without incurring austerity.

3P is the only macroeconomic policy that is based on microeconomic principles and existing market arrangements where price-setting is exercised by companies as opposed to indirectly through monetary aggregates. This makes any direct connection between microeconomics and macroeconomics quite obscure because the underlying monetary theory in the form of the Quantity Theory of Money is misleading.

On the other hand, the Bank of England monetary policy decision track record over the last century is that of cycles of an unstable expansion and contraction of money volumes marked by prejudicial bouts of austerity.

Because, especially since the 1970s, the characteristics of inflation have been cost-push, the use of interest rates to reduce inflation has been highly prejudicial because these intensify the fall in real incomes by adding to costs.

Rather than demand being created by money volume RIO generates demand and consumption by increasing the value of the currency and real incomes by incentivising lower prices for goods and services resulting in real growth as a natural result of the income-price elasticity of demand..

This makes RIO and 3P a distinct macroeconomic paradigm from Keynesian variants, monetarism and SSE.

Keynesianism emerged as a new macroeconomic paradigm 88 years ago and SSE was first proposed 44 years ago. Although RIO was first proposed some 50 years ago and in spite of it being brought to the attention of the main British political parties there was little receptivity as a result of an unjustified over-enthusiasm with Keynesianism or monetarism and a refusal to even consider that an alternative paradigm might exist and serve the country better.

The key and somewhat counter-intuitive operation of RIO and 3P is that there is no emphasis of monetary volumes as a source of demand to create growth but rather a reliance on entrepreneurism that brings about change in technologies and processes to lower unit costs and prices of better goods and services. This was, after all, how much of Britain's industrial revolution and economic growth took place and where several banks were created on the strength of accumulating cash flow of industrial and manufacturing companies.

The Real Incomes Approach can recreate the conditions that drove the industrial revolution by reducing reliance of debt and providing a proactive incentive for sustained rises in productivity, cash flows and real incomes.

RIO and 3P are unique in marrying commercial business rules designed to achieve market penetration and growth with regulations on corporate taxation. Such taxation in the form of the PPL brings to companies the ability to adjust their marketing strategies to trade off risk and margins in a supportive macroeconomic regime.

Keynesian variant, monetarism and SSE provide no such business rules and provide no inherent policy support to companies either through business rules or by permitting a beneficial adaptability of company operations to the maximization of efficiency and the creation of reciprocal value-added transactions and the reduction in zero-sum transactions.

RIO is a quite distinct supply side paradigm and represents an advance in economic theory and practice that is relevant to bringing about a recovery of the British economy.

7. The Implementation of Price Performance Policy (3P)

Using taxation to promote innovation and real growth

The implementation of 3P requires a system that is error and fraud proof to prevent incorrect records or "*creative accounting*" from corrupting data records, a simple and transparent process of administration for companies and a supportive government administrative oversight free from red tape.

The system has to achieve a major impetus to innovation and rising productivity through critical support services which contribute to the understanding and advance in the adoption of state-of-the-art technologies.

No red tape

The system needs to be automated to simplify operations so as to free both companies and government oversight operations from red tape and time-consuming tasks.

Somewhat like personal taxation based on PAYE, PPL is a real time assessment of tax which can reduce or eliminate corporate tax avoidance and evasion.

National Production Systems Service

In order to provide access to a general guidance for corporate management on how the performance of the technologies and techniques used in their companies compares with domestic sector and international performance, an extension system under a suggested name of ***National Production Systems Service (NPSS)*** is proposed as a multisector extension system.

Extension systems gather information and conduct research to establish the ranges of feasible performance of different production and handling systems in any sector, for example in industry and manufacturing.

These have existed in agriculture for many years.

These services integrate information on technologies, engineering and economics and state-of-the-art practice in the most effective deployment of equipment.

To guide those contemplating change to improve performance and profitability, extension systems use analysed field data to provide reports containing data on the relative performance of different types and state-of-the-art processes based on existing systems classified as best, average and poor practice. These are often associated with corresponding gross margins or profitability with such information subject to regular updates, preferably annually, on associated costs so as to remain current and useful.

This has the purpose of assisting managers detect where their own performance is below par and provides information on how to improve performance related to the management of the basic technologies as well as the techniques used by labour to manage operations

The NPSS would be best organized as a partnership between sector companies and universities in order to keep engineering and economic faculties abreast of the state of the art of all nationally and internationally available production technologies as well as identifying areas where possible improvements can be made.

This form of organization is also essential to coordinate and run annual surveys of the state of the art and performance.

For further information on an extension system layout see Annex 5 Extension Systems

Should the NPSS be private or public?

In those cases where I have witnessed public extension systems become private, invariably the advisory officials set up as commission agents to equipment and supplies manufacturers and end up providing imbalanced or biased "advice" to farmers.

To remain independent of this type of bias a public ownership is preferable.

Process reference models-PRMs

The practice performance benchmarks or reference to good, average and poor practice refer to functioning processes with quantitative inputs and realized outputs and operational process flow data. This data includes inputs, production capacity, capacity utilization, working hours each day, and associated product yields (to desired specification) providing the parameters for simple Process Reference Models (PRMs).

These refer to existing systems and therefore what is established to be feasible operational performances.

They can be used by management as modules to build operational models to review options for investment and raised productivity based on simulations.

PPIMS-Price Performance Information Management System

No more creative accounting

A common question concerning 3P, when first discussed more broadly in 1981, is how it can prevent "creative accounting" from undermining the whole process. This usually is made possible by leaving taxation accounts to be prepared by companies or individuals submitting them.

Today it is well within the capabilities of information technology and communications to manage 3P both at the individual corporate level and linked to the level of the government administration.

In a macroeconomic policy environment, the process of administration dealing with data collected on corporate operations requires an integration of a system to collect relevant operational data on inputs and outputs at corporate level but also a treasury function whereby PPL rebates and surcharges are made to a corporate holding account in real time with administrative oversight.

Because of the relative complexity and the risk of mistakes or fraud, it is necessary to build in automation to a standardized computer program that calculates PPRs and PPLs.

The records of both input and sales transactions need to be recorded based on actual transactions making use of separate procurement and sales trading floors where actual transactions are the inputs for recorded data sets.

Trading floors

Trading floors are online interfaces where buyers and sellers can transact on a contractual basis with all of the transacted items being members of agricultural, industrial, and service input and sales object types, each with specifications or properties and object identification tags. Use can be made of object-oriented factors of objects by name and properties (specifications) using existing standardised taxonomies.

Trading floors can be automated along similar lines of how today's large international online sales systems, such as the Amazon.com system, operates.

Procurement trading floor

The trading floor for ***procurement of inputs*** would normally be a business-to-business setup (B2B) with an interface allowing lookup on product specifications and prices where traders wish to view products, or on an automatic basis with buyers setting maximum prices for specific types of input with stated properties and leaving the system to match requests to offers and to close contracts and record details of the transactions.

Sales trading floor

The trading floor for sales of output would be business to business in the case of capital goods and business supplies, but can also be similar to online sales systems wholesales trade and like Amazon.com for final products and services for consumers.

Trade commissions?

The purpose of trading floors is to provide an efficient system for data collection to support 3P. The system would have no commercial transactional fees but could be maintained by a low levy in the form of a sector corporate membership fee.

Trading records and database technology

All of this data can be held in an Accumulog[76] or immutable database for any required audits or oversight and for following up on any forms of dispute.

Modern SQL databases can handle such a large data requirement with ease.

PPRs and PPLs generated from transactional records

Based on the list or menu of components making up units of output in standardized systems and transactional records for each company, it is possible for PPR and PPL estimates to be calculated automatically for set periods established as the periodic estimate duration.

---

76 Accumulogs were identified as an essential requirement for recording online transactions by the author in 1985 while developing locational-state theory at the ITTTF (Brussels) in 1983-1987 as a means of ensuring data transmitted for business decision analysis is reliable. http://www.accumulog.com

Note that PPRs are based on actual input costs and unit output sales records and the PPL "look up tables" would relate to the current regulatory agreements on such things as the respective PPL formulae and basic levy rate B.

Inflationary and deflationary conditions

Following feedback from Robin Matthews in 1981 I added another PPR formula to handle deflationary as opposed to inflationary conditions.

However, today, Boolean logic decision trees can be used to handle quite complex possibilities linked to "look up tables" which set the current PPR values for price setting against unit costs movements.
The general expectation is that if aggregate unit costs rise (inflation), unit output prices should rise but at a lower rate or even decline, if the technologies deployed make this possible. The general expectation is that if aggregate unit costs fall (deflation) unit output prices should also fall. In either case the percentage response of prices to the movement in costs generates the appropriate PPR calculation.

Monitoring of projections against implementation data

As an essential corporate management input, the system needs to provide a means of monitoring the degree to which implemented changes in unit costs compare with the original period projections in unit costs.

This is to enable rapid adjustments to keep PPRs and PPL rates at advantageous values.

Treasury function

The settlement of PPL liability should be an automated real time process that operates on the termination of each assessment period to be decided (somewhat like VAT periods).

Assessment periods will vary with respect to the types of integrated technologies because by their nature, different goods production and service systems can attain different feasible rates of productivity gains and degrees of unit cost reductions.

PPL payments would be credited to a government account.

Performance alert system

The number of surcharge payments and their amounts would be used as indicators to an NPSS alert system indicating issues with a company's performance under 3P related to an inability to lower prices or unit costs activating a query concerning the offer of a consultation to review options to improve performance.

Such monitoring can have a role of identifying constraints in state-of-the-art systems requiring investigation to find ways to improve productivity.

Surcharge recycling

If on assessing non-performance to be due to errors in price setting or technological changes introduced and where credible options exist to achieve price reductions or appropriate technical changes in support of such prices, then the total surcharges made within the previous non

performant year can be returned to the corporate account based on audited use of those funds for the new production plan.
In other cases, the state-of-the art performance reference practice benchmarks might indicate difficulties in processes using specific technologies to deliver desirable gains in unit cost reductions or price reductions.

The task then becomes an investigation to identify subsector applied research and development priorities to be passed to appropriate teams at universities or systems groups by the NPSS.

In the meantime, the PPL formula can be altered for specific classes of state-of-the-art technology facing performance augmentation constraints.

Policy Administration System-PAS

The corporate-level IT systems described would be essentially terminals of an online system with the data centre located at the appropriate government administration for this policy.
In reference to the NPSS data and company activities, a Policy Administration System (PAS) would exercise oversight of two areas which could be linked to National Statistics:

- National performance estimates
- Risk analysis

Corporate privacy

It is to be expected that there could be a reluctance of companies allowing an agency that is concerned with corporate levies to have access to their trading operations data.

There is an example of the European Commission FADN (Farm Accountancy Data Network) and the former UK NAAS (National Agricultural Advisory Network), both of which collect or collected extremely detailed input costs and produce price data and accounts of operational farms. In the UK case, in exchange for optimized farm plans to augment income, each year, the agreements with the farmers were that none of the data in these data sets were to be shared with tax authorities with annual accounts being submitted to the tax authorities by farmers through normal procedures.

Any published data would be anonymized as an average figure for at least five farms falling into a specific size and production systems category.

The whole objective of 3P is to assist companies in lowering their tax obligations as a function of improved efficiency or productivity related to price setting.
In reality, 3P should be viewed as a productivity system designed to help companies excel.

The spirit of the PAS is very much a system attempting to augment corporate performance by catalysing price competition, profitability and a sustained process of innovation.

It is in this spirit that companies need to view 3P.

Information classes

Work with sector panels formed at the Information Technology & Telecommunications Task Force (Brussels) to review the potential contributions of online information to support EU businesses were formed in the early 1980s in [77] the knowledge that the Internet would form the backbone of a global system.

On the question of information sharing, there were three basic classes:

- ***Information disseminated*** to promote the interests of a sector to the public
- ***Shared information*** on state-of-the-art technologies and economic performance benchmarks to assess and guide productivity increases
- ***Confidential information*** of specific in-company techniques and procedures considered to provide a competitive edge, including intellectual property.

It is worth noting that the 3P oversight system dealing with PPR and PPL estimates can make no inroads to gaining access to Confidential information.

National performance estimates

Quarterly reports on sector performance and resulting price stability (inflation) can inform the government and the

[77] McNeill, H. W., *"The use of sector panels in the identification of advanced ICT applications"*, OQSI, DAI, 2015.

Chancellor on whether or not changes in base rates or PPL formulae need to be made.
This is because in some areas of applied technology, the current challenges might be set too high to achieve meaningful improvements in productivity.

Risk analysis and intelligence

Risk analysis and intelligence refers to the detection of problems with the operation and oversight of the system and work on the degree of progress of some sectors towards achieving internationally comparative performance to expand import substitution and exports.

Introduction of the system

Because of the nature of British partisan politics, changing any system concerning changes in macroeconomic policies and their administration carries with it political risks which can be reduced through an adequate explanation of the specific mutual and distributed benefits to business, consumers and the workforce alike.
The central point is to show a drive to develop a positive systemic consistency to avoid opposition driving the "debate" to where things get out of control. An example of this was the attempt to introduce as innocent a policy instrument community charge, referred to as the "Poll tax". As a result of an inadequate preparation and quantitative analysis within any due diligence applied the negative impacts in 1990 led to street violence.

It is suggested that the introduction of 3P should be first of all, a voluntary scheme rather than an attempt to commit to the system for the whole country.

There is a need to assess how the system works and its ability to reduce inflation on a reduced scale, as well as debug the corporate and central administration of the system.

Obvious candidates are sectors with a few large operators, such as energy and utilities.

Likely evolution

In theory, those volunteering to operate under a 3P scheme should find that they become more competitive than those who remain under existing corporate taxation schemes. If so, the number of volunteers joining the scheme should grow.

Wage contracts and settlements

Despite the reduction of inflation and likelihood of specific technological processes being able to reduce prices, such as in digital technologies, the purchasing power of the pound and therefore the real wages should rise. However, given the importance of human learning to increases in productivity, 3P could create a basis for PPL rebates being considered to be bonuses to be shared between companies and the labour force.

If the 3P results in a substantive rise in the purchasing power of the currency, there is the option to introduce schemes where labour shares PPL rebates at the same rate as companies over and above the base rate being paid as bonuses.

As a result, there are two positive components to real income rises. One is the general rise in real incomes associated with the reduction in inflation and the other is, depending upon employment arrangements, bonuses based on PPL rebates.

Mutual and cooperative companies

Mutual and cooperative groups can benefit from 3P because their members are shareholders and therefore would benefit directly from a 3P scheme. Mutual and cooperative structures, because they do not have external shareholders or shareholder value targets, benefit from an estimated 11%-15% operational costs advantage, and 3P can help lever this benefit, especially in the case of smaller companies.

In this case, the 3P rebates can benefit the "workforce" directly.

More for less productivity

More for less signifies fewer resources consumed to produce a product or service, and this provides a foundation for the stimulation of the types of technologies that are more conducive to resource conservation and ecological balance as baseline states to tackle climate change related to rising temperatures.

Climate action, the environment and ecosystem and planetary carrying capacity

Just as there are business rules for increasing productivity and reducing or eliminating inflation, so there is an important additional set of business operational criteria that needs to address the climate crisis and ecosystem preservation.

3P business rules and the environmental challenge

There has been much media coverage of the high cost of introducing what people refer to as the "Green Agenda", referring to red tape and regulations apparently throttling companies and threatening business viability.

3P business rules support decision analysis on changes in technology in the appropriate direction in terms of environmental protection, but in each case consideration of environmental impacts is, of course, required.

It is not altogether apparent, beyond a well-informed business community, why addressing climate change and ecological and environmental preservation is such a challenge.

In many cases, it appears to be an excuse not to do anything but to allow the current state of affairs to approach a point of no return and post a global threat to society.
It is proposed that given the complexity of handling specific technological questions about the specific impacts of different technologies on the environment, the proposed National Production Systems Service (NPSS) should place particular emphasis on this aspect of productivity decisions.

Indeed, with the introduction of more exacting environmental regulations in the European Union, it became necessary to introduce an advisory system to help farmers understand and apply them.

Across all sectors, this is more of a challenge covering all types of technologies, and for this reason there is a need to try and establish a centre capable of handling these types of questions.

The George Boole Foundation initiated a quest to address these questions in 2010 under the Decision Analysis Initiative 2010-2020. This gave rise to the Open Quality Standards Initiative (OQSI), which developed practical procedural methods to assist companies in completing a critical path analysis that helps decide the appropriateness of any technological decision.

OBAs are options benefit analyses similar to cost benefit analysis, but they work in a reciprocal fashion to determine economic rates of return (ERR) or rate of return to the environment (RRE).

Thus, OBA1 is a standard cost-benefit analysis; OBA2 is a cost-benefit analysis based on social viability and real incomes; OBA3 is environmental/ecosystem impact analysis; OBA4 is the resultant climate (emissions) and carrying capacity impacts.

The basic changes in technology and processes are subject to performance criteria similar to the OECD DAC criteria, only OQSI added the additional criterion of resilience as a measure to help avoid sustainability being undermined by varying economic or natural conditions. The OQSI Critical Path is shown below[78].

---

[78] McNeill H. W., Parts 1 and 2, "*Project and macroeconomic coherence for Agenda 2030 Sustainable Development Goals*", Agricultural Innovation, 2020

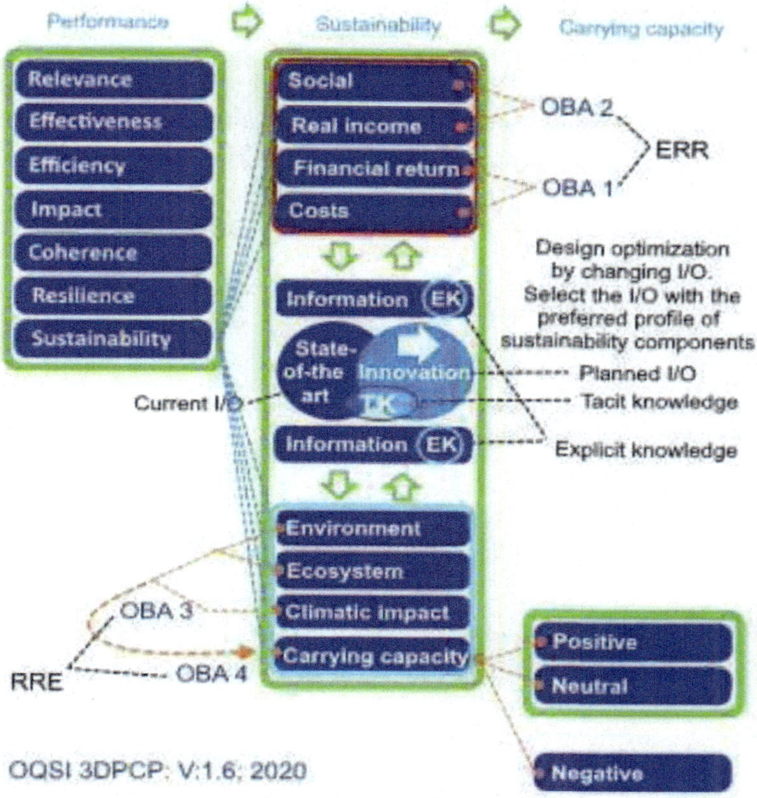

OQSI Critical Path

The performance criteria for any specific objective (production and sales of a good or service) are therefore:

- Relevance to objective
- Effectiveness in achieving objective
- Efficiency in achieving objective
- Actual expected impact
- Coherence with policy objective and other actions
- Resilience of variations in conditions in markets and environment

- Overall sustainability

The OBAs essentially assess sustainability of options covering the following sustainability criteria:

- Social
- Real income
- Financial return
- Costs
- The technical change option
- Environment
- Ecosystem
- Climatic impact
- Carrying capacity

As can be seen throughout this assessment, a matter of mutual existential interest is the need to assess the appropriateness of different technological options centred around more-for-less production systems identified applying the 3P business rules.

Technologies are adjusted in a reiterative fashion according to the feedback information (explicit knowledge) from the two assessments of economic rates of return (ERR) and rates of return to the environment (RRE).

Any change that ends up with a negative carrying capacity is rejected.

The critical path to be followed remains within the green boundaries.

The OQSI Critical Path can be applied to analyse changes in any production system.

Concluding

This document has explained the shortcomings of monetary policy in terms of flaws in the Quantity Theory of Money (QTM) with reference to an alternative Value Theory of Money[79] used to explain why decisions based on the QTM have resulted in an inability to eliminate inflation while imposing reductions in real incomes.

Over the last 50 years, this has resulted in deindustrialization, falling investment and inadequate productivity gains, falling real incomes, rising income disparity and poverty, rising imports and a large negative balance of payments in goods.

A proposition, in the form of a Price Performance Policy (3P), has been presented as a way to accelerate a return to real growth based on unit price reductions in goods and services and a sustained policy traction of promoting rising productivity. The productivity structure under 3P is a more-for-less transition as opposed to the confusion of money volumes or aggregate demand as generators of inflationary relatively unproductive and wasteful "growth".

A general description of a corporate and national administration system for 3P has been outlined.

---

79 http://www/boolean.org.uk/library/Theories_of_Money.pdf

Annex 1

Productivity

Productivity has been referred to frequently in this book.

This annex is a short guide to:

1. What productivity is
2. How is it measured
3. Its role in advancing growth in real incomes 4. The different ways in which productivity increases
5. What is more-for-less?

1. What is productivity?

Productivity is a measure of the efficiency with which a combination of resources are used to create a product. It is a relationship between outputs and inputs.

2. How is productivity measured?

For a long time, productivity has been measured in terms of how many units of output an hour are produced by two standard inputs. One is labour-hour input and the other is output secured using all factors used referred to as total factor productivity.

So, these are:

1. Output per labour hour
2. Output per all factor inputs

The number of output units can be multiplied by unit prices to obtain the productivity measured in terms of value of output expressed in pounds for each type of standard input.

3. Productivity's role in increasing real incomes

Over time, largely as a result of human learning, productivity or the relationship between output and input changes with more physical units being produced by labour hours or by all factor inputs.

Besides learning, productivity can rise as a result of changes in technology used. These changes mean more units and a higher value is produced per standard input. This can result in a reduction of unit costs enabling a reduction in unit prices thereby increasing the purchasing power of the currency for that particular product. This results in the purchasing power of a nominal income rising thereby raising real incomes.

Why rising productivity often fails to raise real incomes and growth

The common bases for measuring productivity include ***output per worker hour*** or total factor productivity.

Under cost-push inflationary conditions, real income rises resulting from such physical measures are not readily apparent. This is because the combination of relative dimensioning of profits and rising costs tends to be determined by anticipatory pricing, which causes a company to be able to maintain profits or even increase them at the expense of consumer real incomes.

However, the only convenient way to measure productivity in a way that conveys a useful message concerning its impact on real incomes, under cost-push inflation and conditions of anticipatory pricing is to determine the Price Performance Ratio (PPR), which is a direct measure of the degree of containment of input inflation in output prices. As a result this provides an estimate of the efficiency with which a company contributes to consumer, and therefore, workforce real incomes.

Naturally, this measure is only relevant when macroeconomic management is a Price Performance Policy (3P) because this is the only policy to maintain the incentive for companies to maintain competitive prices based on their PPR setting.

Without the 3P macroeconomic framework and incentives, the notion of price productivity remains without any logic.

Real productivity

Real productivity has a connotation whereby Real Incomes policies aim to sustain a ***positive systemic consistency*** of transactions characterized by mutual benefit, or reciprocal value-added, in contrast to the notion of zero-sum. The counterintuitive aspect to this is that this approach is designed to help companies maximize their incomes and market share as well as profits subject to the feasible changes in innovation and technical productivity.

Productivity measured in terms of gradual progress in increasing the ratio of physical output to physical inputs involving changes in technology and techniques, the way humans apply technology, occurs as the result of a combination of factors.

4. The different ways in which productivity increases

Production systems combine technologies with variable inputs, energy, information and people.

Since humans manage technology but also contribute directly to productivity by their unaided actions they have a vital role in advancing productivity associated with

1. Tacit knowledge
2. Explicit knowledge

In terms of technology, there are seven main types of productivity that can be used to improve the performance of processes into which people are integrated.

These include:

1. Capital-embodied productivity
2. Capital-disembodied productivity (including explicit knowledge)
3. Learning curve
4. Automation
5. Scale
6. Resources utilization
7. Shop floor innovation

5. What is more-for-less?

More for less signifies a reduction in the physical menu of inputs used to create or build a unit of output.

As will be noticed in all of the following examples of sources of productivity the general result in the consumption of less resources to create a desired result.

How this is arrived at varies with the type of productivity effect varying from packing more logic into physically smaller lower energy consuming integrated circuits to the use of process design to gradually reduce if not eliminate waste and raising production system yields to close to 100%. Zerodefect manufacturing is usually considered to be the target on more-for-less but invariably break-throughs in technology and design change the underlying process to achieve even more-from-less.

Human capabilities

Human capabilities and roles within production systems can be related to two types of knowledge[80]:

1. Tacit knowledge
2. Explicit knowledge

1. Tacit knowledge

Tacit knowledge is the capabilities that each person accumulates as a result of experience and the repetition of specific tasks so it combines physical coordination and intellectual capabilities based on learning.

However, tacit knowledge is very difficult to pass on to others because it is the result of each person going through their own learning process.

---

[80] McNeill, H. W. "*Tacit & Explicit Knowledge*", Real Incomes, 2000. McNeill, H. W., "*Technology, technique and real Incomes*", Charter House Essays in Political Economy, HPC, 2021.

A simple example is that of riding a bicycle where providing an explanation of what each part of the bike is for does not teach the person how to ride and maintain balance. The person needs to go down this "learning curve" themselves.

Tacit knowledge is characterised by the fact that practice improves is significance and a person's capabilities.

2. Explicit knowledge

Explicit knowledge is essentially the sum total of knowledge expressed as written and oral symbology or language and communications including mathematics, logic and deterministic cause and effect relationships.
Unlike tacit knowledge, explicit knowledge is easier to pass on to others and is essentially the main means of communicating knowledge between people and in instruction.
Explicit knowledge has an important role in recording events and progress in such things as productivity to support analysis and discovering ways to improve future operations.

Technological productivities

1. Capital-embodied productivity

Capital-embodied productivity is gains in process efficiency arising from embedded mechanics or logic modules, such as an integrated circuit or a catalytic converter in an internal combustion engine.

Digital technologies

A particular area in which advances have had a deflationary impact on products is digital technologies.

Very much linked to Moore's Law[81] or the ability to pack increasing amounts of digital logic onto smaller substrates or integrated circuits. This results in smaller logical or decision-making packages consuming less material, less energy and less space and incurring lower unit costs.

As a result, digital devices have been characterized by offering more energy efficiency, compactness and power per currency unit.

In real terms, most digital devices tend to be on a deflationary and consumer-beneficial trend, with prices falling over time.

Biomedical technologies

Another area where there is a very large potential for deflationary impacts on products and services is the advances in biomedical or life sciences.

Techniques making use of DNA decoding and coding and stem cell regenerative properties are opening up a wide range of potential medical and agricultural application to replace expensive operations and reconstructive surgery interventions.

---

[81] Moore, G. E., "Cramming more components onto integrated circuits", Electronics, Volume 38, Number 8, April 19, 1965

Much of the active components are simply natural determinant relationships whose operations have been uncovered just in the last 50 years.

Logic

Explicit knowledge, especially in the area of specific knowledge domains can be represented, analysed and recreated through the application of logic. The ubiquitous logic used in most digital applications including hardware and software is Boolean or binary logic developed by George Boole and set out in his 1854 book, "*The Laws of Thought*"[82].

Boole did not develop his logic for computers or programming but developed his mathematic logic to explain how humans deduce by observing events, cause and effect relationships and the probabilities of events to make decisions. Increasingly complex algorithms or scripts based on Boolean logic are automating complex decisions and analyses in such areas as law, finance as well as in decision analysis models used to review all feasible options to resolve specific problems including economic policy options.

This evolution is significantly increasing the productivity of such service tasks and reducing the costs of complex services and eroding the high income end of the services sector with the development of DIY applications.

2. Capital-disembodied productivity

Capital-disembodied gains in productivity arise from the application of decision analysis to determine how a

---

[82] "*George Boole*", The George Boole Foundation Limited website.

production system operates and how resources and time are allocated. For example, operations research techniques such as linear programming[83] can be used to optimize the use of resources in production lines or multi-product line enterprises like farms with multiple crop and animal production lines or in ingredient purchasing in feed mix operations to minimize the cost of completed products.

A benefit of capital-disembodied productivity gains is that they often do not require significant investment in plant, but usually such optimization is applied to fixed capital in what is termed short-term planning. As a result, cost-benefit to such efforts can be high.

The advent of "Apps" has given rise to ways to increase the efficiency of specific tasks for personal and professional use, saving time and providing precision and accuracy in calculation where needed.

3. Learning curve

The aeronautical engineer Theodore Wright [84] and the economists Nicholas Kaldor[83], Kenneth Arrow[85] and Robert

---

[83] Dorfman, R., Samuelson, P., Solow, R. M., "*Linear Programming & Economic Analysis*", Rand Corp., McGraw-Hill 1958.

[84] Wright, T., "Factors Affecting the Cost of Airplanes" (Journal of Aeronautical Science, Volume 3, No.2, 1936, pp. 122-128). [83] Kaldor, N., "A Model of Economic Growth", The Economic Journal, Volume 67, Issue 268, Pages 591-624, 1957.

[85] Arrow, K. J., "The economic implications of learning by doing". The Review of Economic Studies. Oxford Journals. 29 (3): 155-73, 1962 [85] Solow, R. M., "Technical change and the aggregate production function". Review of Economics and Statistics.

Solow[85] made significant contributions to show the how changes in technology combined with "learning on the job" by undertaking repetitive functions leads to fewer production mistakes, faster execution, less waste and a higher yield in terms of saleable output and a reduction in resources used per product, leading to a reduction in unit costs of production. The greater the throughput of production, the greater the gains from learning. This process is referred to as the learning curve.

The majority of the learning is undertaken by the workforce and the combination of a workforce with a specific set of technology creates characteristic learning curves associated with the acquisition of capabilities and increasing competence of those employed.

Learning curve characteristics

For any particular process, there is a quantifiable reduction in unit costs of production as throughput increases.

This can be used to construct accurate projections of likely future unit costs of production.

A reasonable heuristic (rule of thumb) guide based on a large range of different production processes has shown that the reduction in unit costs tends to be a constant percentage drop in unit costs, which is associated with each doubling of cumulative historic production throughput.

The percentage drop in unit costs is referred to as the learning curve coefficient (LCC).

---

(3): 312-20 ,1957.

Notice that the learning curve demonstrates diminishing marginal returns to throughput over time indicated by the slope of the learning curve unit costs line becoming less inclined (flatter).

For example, the table below shows the unit cost profile of a 20% LCC.

Excellent coverages of the learning curve have been provided by Belkaoui[86], Hirschmann[87] and Nagy[88] et al.

A 20% learning curve coefficient calculation

Cumulative historic throughout	Percentage reduction	Unit costs
100	0%	45.0
200	20%	36.0
400	20%	28.8
800	20%	23.0
1600	20%	18.4
3200	20%	14.7

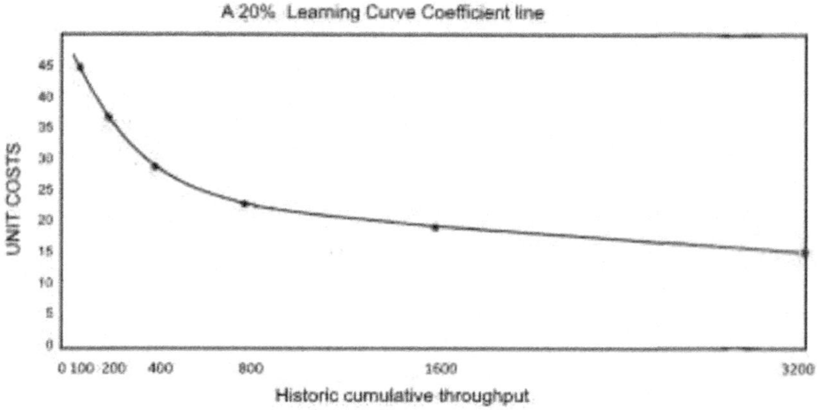

4. Automation

Automation is an important way of gaining productivity, progressing from past mechanical systems[89] through to computer assisted[86] and today to digital logic and controls used to introduce deductive logic and decision making[91] into systems' controls based on software or integrated circuits referred to variously as 5th Generation, Digital Logic or Artificial Intelligence (AI).

---

[86] Arden, B. W., *"What can be Automated?"*, The Computer Science and Engineering Research Study (COSERS), MIT Press, 1980. [91] McNeill, H. W., *"The State of the Art and Future of Decision Analysis"*, SEEL-Systems Engineering Economics Lab, George Boole Foundation Limited, 2020.

86 Belkaoui, A., "The Learning Curve - A Management Accounting Tool", Quorum Books, 1986.

87 Hirschmann, w. B., "Learning Curve", Chemical Engineering (Volume 71, No. 7,1964) pp 95-100.

88 Bela Nagy, J. Doyne Farmer, Quan M. Bui and Jessika E Trancik. "Statistical Basis for Predicting Technological Progress", 2012, Santa Fe Institute, 1399 Hyde Park Road, Santa Fe, NM 87501, USA, St. John's College,1160 Camino Cruz Blanca, Santa Fe, NM, 87505, USA and Engineering Systems Division, Massachusetts Institute of Technology, Cambridge, MA, 02139, USA.

89 Giedion, S., "*Mechanization Takes Command - a contribution to anonymous history*", Oxford University Press, 1948.

With the advent of the World Wide Web and advanced generations of telecommunications technologies, the control of processes has begun to include an almost real-time remote control of industrial and even surgical procedures carried out by remote surgeons, as well as the coordination of driverless transport platoons.

Besides these physical processes, digital logic implemented in software or integrated circuits has already begun to automate trading activities, legal document generation and financial trading decisions as well as in the field of strategic planning.

As a result, many top-end service sector posts are being replaced by automation, and the ubiquitous international nature of information technology capabilities and programming competence means that the earning abilities in many "specialized" service professions is likely to be on the decline as automation takes over a significant part of such professional effort.

Automation introduces stepwise drops in unit costs if well selected and designed. This results in discontinuities in the learning curve. With each increment of automation added to different areas of a process the learning curve is interrupted and then the learning curve coefficient continues to have effect but often at a different rate of unit costs reduction.

5. Scale

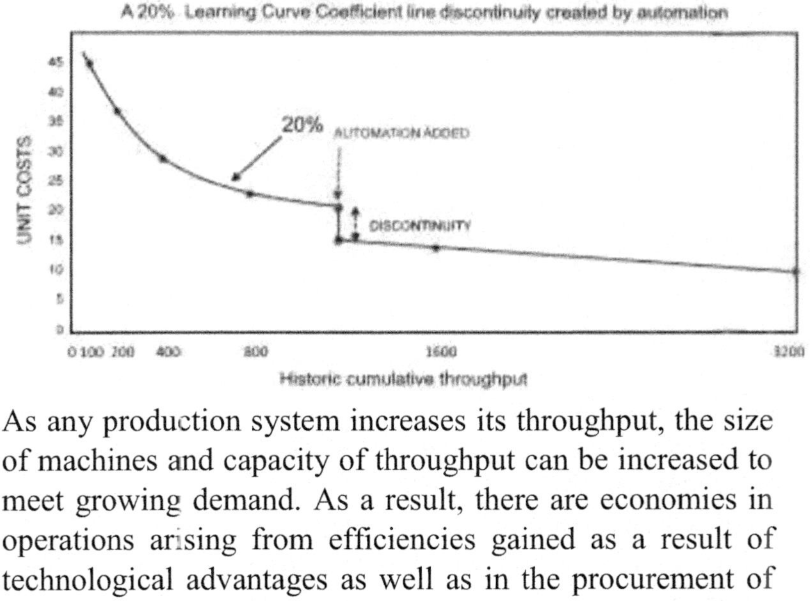

As any production system increases its throughput, the size of machines and capacity of throughput can be increased to meet growing demand. As a result, there are economies in operations arising from efficiencies gained as a result of technological advantages as well as in the procurement of larger volumes of inputs and sales where transactional bargaining power increases.

At the same time, handling large volumes in well-designed plants contributes to reductions in operational costs.

If plant is designed and developed and implemented to possess a larger capacity it is often a case of multiplying standard processes or adding larger processes which gain lower unit costs and unit curve discontinuities similar to automation impacts on the learning curve.

6. Resources utilization

Resources utilization combines measures of throughput capacity, capacity utilization and production yield compared with total input costs to calculate unit costs of final output.

This relationship underlies the Learning Curve and Scale of Operations.

So, unit costs are represented by:

UC = TC/(C x Ct x Cs x Y

Where:

UC is unit costs;
TC is total costs of inputs;
C is maximum capacity of throughout/day;
Ct is time operational per day;
Cs is system settings (speed, power);
Y is yield or percentage of output up to saleable specification.

The minimum unit cost (UC) with a total cost of 30,000 and operating at full capacity (300/day) and with a yield of 100% would be 100.

30,000/300 x 1.00 x 1.00 x 1.00) = 100

A low yield indicates waste either in the form of materials used and an inability to sell a proportion of output not up to the required specification. Low operational times and equipment settings imply lower output per day. This would be associated with higher unit costs associated with fixed overheads and workforce.

Zero defect manufacturing involves maintaining at Yields at 100%.

7. Shop floor innovation

Shop floor innovation (SFI)[87] refers to spontaneous ad hoc innovations arising from operators coming up with suggestions on how to improve a process. This is an important source of advancing economies and is connected to the learning curve process but occurring in a disjointed fashion while gaining unit costs reductions.

Innovation and entrepreneurship

The process of technological advance or innovation leading to economic growth was established and reconfirmed by several economists while the work of Theodore Wright and later by Kenneth Arrow' confirmed that the main driver of such innovation is "*Learning by doing*" leading to advances in enquiry and the investigation to identify ways to improve the efficiency and convenience of tasks to achieve specific ends.

---

87 McNeill H. W., "*A constitutional economic policy - Part 7 Designing a sustainable future - Step 1*", Real Incomes

What is innovation?

Innovation is defined as occurring when a task used to create a specific output is changed to another process for the first time [88] in a specific location. Usually innovation is associated with improvements in efficiency or productivity. Notice that from the standpoint of economics and economic development, innovation has a locational-state[89] reference signifying that what is innovation at a specific time in a specific location might well be something already in operation in another location signifying that it has been in operations from some time in the past.

The human intervention and management of this process is referred to as entrepreneurship.

The diffusion of innovation

By far the most important means of the spread of innovation over geographic space is by ***technology transfer*** either through emulation but more usually through the sale of more advanced technologies and products as part of trade between regions and countries.

Technology transfer is among the most rapid means of spreading productivity worldwide. The concept of an extension system of the proposed National Production Systems Service (NPSS) has the role in accelerating the rate

---

[88] Mansfield E., "*The Economics of Technological Change*" W. W. Norton & Co. Inc, 1968

[89] McNeill, H. W., "*The State of the Art and Future of Decision Analysis*", DAI, George Boole Foundation, 2012, McNeill, H. W., "*Locational-State Theory*", DAI, George Boole Foundation, 2013.

of take up of state-of-the-art technologies and adoption of good practice.

Accelerating Innovation and Real economic growth

One of the seldom commented upon functions of extension systems and the proposed NPSS is the function of accelerating innovation and real economic growth.

The simple process of making people aware of a new costs-saving technology that works and providing sufficient information for a potential used to take a decision to use it can help accelerate real economic growth.

So, the diagram below shows the impact of shortening the time to a higher rate of sector take up of a new technology reduces the time when a higher percentage of sector user are operating at a higher level of productivity. This signifies that a larger proportion of economic units within a sector can take more advantage of the benefits offered by a macroeconomic environment such as 3P.

Calculating the real growth impact

Based on technological categories which consist of "technical packages" of a set of defined and equipment and the levels of competence of labour in using the appropriate techniques based on proven practice (poor, average and good) established for the process concerned, it is possible to calculate the potential rise in real productivity in a sector by recording the growth in such processes being implemented in a sector and brought up to operational status each year.

Baseline productivity

One of the problems with the Bank of England "target" inflation rate reduces the rate of economic growth arising from what is known as baseline productivity.

Even without the effort of introducing RIO 3P the baseline productivity across all economic sectors is around 2% on average and has remained near to that since 1945. However, the target inflation rate of 2% results in this causing real growth to remain as 0%. By eliminating inflation something

Accelerating real growth through enhanced diffusion of state of the art technology

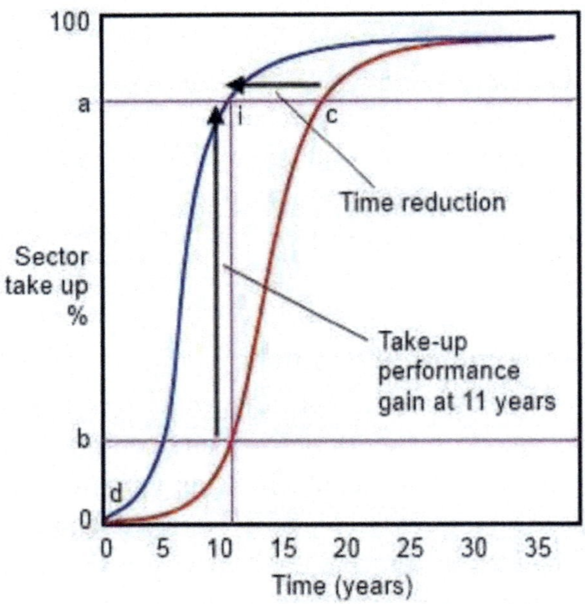

Diffusion of technology

like a real growth in real incomes would in 2024 be around £56 billion or 2% of the GDP.

Jean-Baptiste Say

The French economist Jean-Baptiste Say[90] (1767-1832) not only saw the significance of supply-side efficiency and

volumes of production in determining aggregate wages and disposable incomes in raising demand in an economy, he also recognized the vital role of entrepreneurship in advancing this growth of the economy through increases in productivity.

Somewhat like Nicholas Kaldor Say did not define entrepreneurs as tycoons and wizards but rather as anyone in any trade with the wit to recognise there were better ways of achieving tasks to end up with lower cost, less waste and resulting in an improve product or service.

Thus, a decline in unit prices help drive consumption as a result of the income-price elasticity of consumption and a rise in real incomes because purchasing power is a function of unit prices.

If unit prices fall real growth occurs as consumption increases.

Note that this is a function of productivity and not of money volumes creating demand and growth.

---

[90] Jean-Baptiste Say, "*A Treatise on Political Economy – The Production, Distribution and Consumption of Wealth*", 1821. [95] Wright, T., "Factors Affecting the Cost of Airplanes" (Journal of Aeronautical Science, Volume 3, No.2, 1936, pp. 122-128). [96] Kaldor, N., "A Model of Economic Growth", The Economic Journal, Volume 67, Issue 268, pp. 591-624, 1957.

Say, before and after the Crash

Before the New York Stock Exchange Crash in 1929 and the advent of the Great Depression, New Deal and John Maynard Keynes' "*General Theory*" the model of the economy expounded by Jean-Baptiste Say was considered to be the rational explanation for the operation of the economy on the part of most economists. Many institutions in the USA had implored Say to go to the USA to help disseminate the logic of his approach but Say preferred to remain in France. It is notable that following the financial crises of the 1930s the most vital element of economic growth, innovation and technological advance and increasing productivity virtually vanished from the considerations of economists as represented by Keynesianism and monetarism.

John Maynard Keynes invested some energy, as did others, in attempting to blame the "Say model" for the possibility of a fall in demand in creating the Depression. What became a tedious academic discussion rotated around what was called Say's Law that "Supply creates its own Demand" which misdirected attention into a barren academic discussion and away from the vital practical role of innovation and productivity and the income-price elasticity of demand as the catalyst for real economic growth under counter inflationary conditions.

However, others blame Keynes for misunderstanding Say's logic[91]. Certainly, reviewing the past academic discussion around Say's Law, it is notable that the dominance of academic economists in continuing this debate resulted in the effective removal of the vital role of innovation and productivity from the Keynesian and general postKeynesian macroeconomic landscape.

However, Wright[95], Kaldor[96], Arrow [9293] and Solow[98] all contributed to the collection of evidence which demands a revisit to Say's logic and in providing a foundation for RIO as a workable paradigm which constitutes a non-monetary counter-inflationary supply side solution to real growth.

The key measure of real economic growth

National innovation strategies

Any company can measure its own PPR and as a result determine where the company is located on a PPR map.
The diagram below is a PPR map which shows an array of PPR values for different input cost and unit output prie changes.

---

91 Kates, S., "*Say's Law and the Keynesian Revolution – How Macroeconomic Theory Lost its Way*", Edward Elgar Publishing, 1998.

92 Arrow, K. J., "The economic implications of learning by doing". The Review of Economic Studies. Oxford Journals. 29 (3): 155-73,
93 . 98 Solow, R. M., "Technical change and the aggregate production function". Review of Economics and Statistics.
(3): 312-20 ,1957.

Under 3P companies need to at least have a PPR of unity (=1.00) and anything above this would be located in the grey area.

Companies can adjust their productivity projections to secure desired unit cost levels to become more competitive and enjoy PPL rebates as the more competitively-prices products and services are distributed in the market gaining market share.

Therefore, it is possible for national innovation strategies to be based on following downward movements in the value of PPRs. The advantage of this approach is that it is transparent and the business rules associated with 3Pparticiption can help companies move in this direction of increasing productivity

Price Performance Ratio Map

Unit input costs	Unit output price change %								
change %	-20	-15	-10	-5	0	5	10	15	20
20	This area represents the innovation target zone					0.25	0.50	0.75	1.00
15						0.33	0.66	1.00	
10						0.50	1.00		
5						1.00			
0					1.00				
-5	0.25	0.33	0.50	1.00					
-10	0.50	0.66	1.00						
-15	0.75	1.00							
-20	1.00								

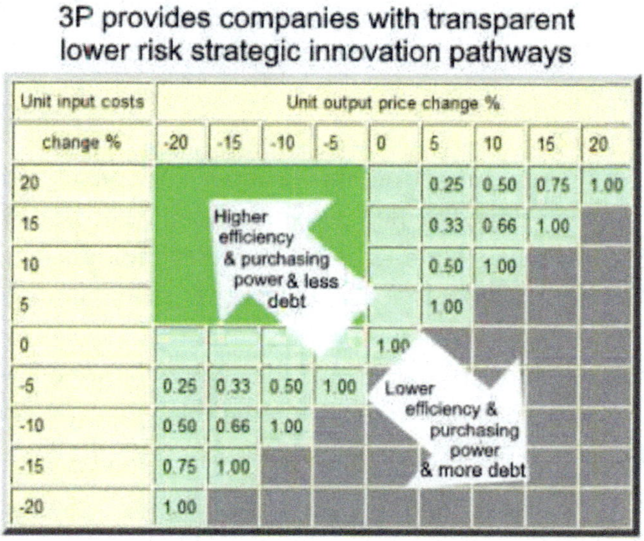

Unit input costs	Unit output price change %								
change %	-20	-15	-10	-5	0	5	10	15	20
20						0.25	0.50	0.75	1.00
15						0.33	0.66	1.00	
10						0.50	1.00		
5						1.00			
0					1.00				
-5	0.25	0.33	0.50	1.00					
-10	0.50	0.66	1.00						
-15	0.75	1.00							
-20	1.00								

The basic requirements

In 1966, Nicholas Kaldor, in his inaugural lecture [94] as Professor of Economics at Cambridge University emphasized the role of industry and manufacturing as an essential component of the evolving British economic productivity as an appeal to ensure that the country maintained a policy to ensure its survival.

His main emphasis was on the role industry and manufacturing had in innovation and in advancing

[94] N. Kaldor. "Causes of the Slow Rate of Economic Growth of the United Kingdom". An Inaugural Lecture. London, Cambridge University Press, 1966, 40 p.,

technological capabilities as a source of better products and processes able to provide all other sectors of the economy with the products and equipment required to advance productivity in all sectors through the diffusion of innovation[95].

Besides this vital function, this process was considered to be one that maintained skilled higher paid jobs that would adapt to the advancing state of the art of technologies through accumulated tacit knowledge and use of explicit knowledge..

Nicholas Kaldor argued against the switch to monetarism by the government in 1975, predicting the erosion in competitivity of the British economy and predicting the current state of the economy.

Annex 2
Legislation assisting financialization

The activities, processes and products of financialization have become an increasingly complex process to the degree that oversight for risk has sometimes been deficient for extremely large amounts of funds.

---

[95] Rogers, E. M., "*Diffusion of Innovations*", Free Press, 1965-2003.

The main contributory steps and phases initiated in the 1970s in the form of changes in mechanisms, techniques and policy are listed below[96] in roughly chronological order:

1. The movement off the Gold standard in 1971 (Nixon, USA)
2. The accelerating development of financial derivative products beyond commodity futures
3. The development of the 1973 Black-Scholes hedging model for derivatives
4. The Reagan administration's generation of one of the largest government debts in history under a monetarist agenda aiming to "reduce the size of government"
5. The rupture of the Glass-Steagall Act (1933) in 1991 when the Commodity Futures Trading Commission provided Goldman Sachs with a "Bona Fide Hedging" exemption to be followed by similar exemptions for other banks
6. Under President Bill Clinton bank deregulation was formalized through the repeal of the Glass-Steagall Act (1933) in 1999 by the Gramm-Leach-Bliley Act. This effectively removed the barrier between retail and investment/trading activities in banks
7. In the UK the Thatcher government deregulated deposit takers, such as mutuals, to become banks on the plc model
8. The dominance of macroeconomic policy by monetarism since the 1975

[96] McNeill, H.W., "*The journey from 1971 to 2020 – the consolidation of financialization*", Real Incomes, 2020.

9. Monetary policy has maintained a tolerance of low but positive inflation rates that have devalued the pound by over 97% since 1945

10. A refusal of policymakers to target zero or negative inflation but maintenance of low positive interest rates creating a real income depreciation treadmill

11. The organization of the Euro Zone in 1999 precipitating and crystallizing economic regional differentials and in some cases national marginalization

12. A rate of enlargement of the European Union since 2004 exceeded the economic resources to bring all countries into a comparable economic status on the basis of the monetarist model applied within the Euro Zone as well as in member states not members of the Euro Zone

13. The increasing participation of banks in derivative and commodity futures trading

14. Bank and company regulation came under extraconstitutional regimes that effectively were managed by the main players in the financial and corporate sector

15. With deregulation and the advance in shaping of many new financial derivative products, private banking activities shifted from their prime policy role as mainstream lenders in support of the social and economic constituency to trading activities including acquisition of assets such as land and property, carried out largely for the benefit of bank shareholders and executives

16. Monetary policy control over national finance has become increasingly ineffective as a result of unrecorded derivative trading being variously reported to be multiples of the size of the national income

17. The growth in the use of performance "ratings" sector based almost exclusively on financial measures and

issued by agencies close to the parties who derive a direct benefit from the sale of dubiously rated products

18. In November 2007 the Federal Reserve in the USA increased interest rates causing many low-income mortgage payers to be unable to meet payments causing many mortgage-based derivatives to lose their value

19. Many banks failed not only because of the falling value of their derivative portfolios but because it became impossible to recoup full equity in collateral because of falling house prices and facing falling dollar exchange rate, exacerbating value of derivatives held by UK banks

20. Governments (2008-2012) decided to bail out banks to such a degree that issues of risk to sovereign debt became a major issue for the social constituencies in terms of future tax liabilities

21. The enforced Euro Zone monetary policy begins to fail in the periphery of Europe where major bank failures and sovereign debt becomes a major issue (Greece, Spain, Portugal, Italy, Cyprus and others) requiring bailouts.

22. Countries enter a phase of low interest rates and quantitative easing hurting savers

23. Austerity regimes initiated to pay off government debts and account deficits exacerbating ability to generate growth

24. Quantitative easing causes a major inflation in the asset markets including land, real estate, precious metals, objects of rare art, selected commodities and shares whose prices are driven upwards by companies using cheap finance to buy back shares)

25. 2020: Flaws in financial/monetary theory exposed and Value Theory of Money established.

Annex 3
Examples of Price Performance Levies

The Real Incomes Approach provides for a very large range of options for applying PPLs to aggregate incomes according to the PPR. The two types are discussed below. The basic calculation of PPLs is to apply a corrective coefficient based on the PPR value to a Basic Levy expressed as a percentage e.g. 20%.

PPL Power functions – intensifications

When policymakers wish to change the intensity of size of the incentive to lower PPRs, a power function can be used to calculate the PPL coefficient. Thus, the table below shows the effect of different PPR power functions on the size of the Levy to be applied to operational margins with a basic levy of 20%:

Some Price Performance Levy Power Functions

Some PPL power functions applied to a basic levy of 20%
The percentages indicate the levy to be paid according to the respective PPR
For comparison a conventional tax or flat tax can be assumed to be 20%

	PPR power function					
	PPR¹		PPR²		PPR³	
PPR	PPL%	net aY%	PPL%	net aY%	PPL%	net aY%
0.00	0.00%	100.00%	0.00%	100.00	0.00%	100.00%
0.25	5.00%	95.00%	1.25%	98.75%	0.31%	99.69%
0.50	10.00%	90.00%	5.00%	95.00%	2.50%	97.50%
0.75	15.00%	85.00%	11.25%	88.75%	8.44%	91.56%
1.00	20.00%	80.00%	20.00%	80.00%	20.00%	80.00%
1.25	25.00%	75.00%	31.25%	68.75%	39.06%	60.94%

Key:	Benefit	(green)	Flat tax	(grey)	Prejudice	(red)

Price Performance Levies based on PPR power functions & net incomes

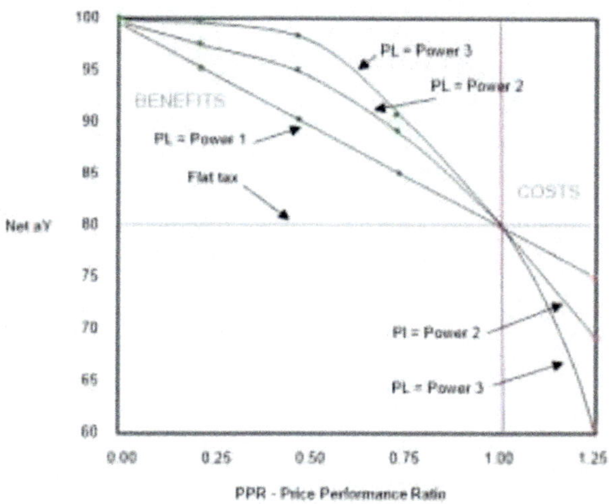

PPL Slide functions – linear reductions or augmentations

Slide functions simply add or deduct from the basic levy value in proportion to the PPR achieved.

The examples below show a basic levy of 20% weighted up or down by 0.25 to generate the PPL value.

Some Price Performance Levy Slide Functions

Some i-d functions applied to a basic levy of 20%
The percentages indicate the levy to be paid according to the respective PPR
For comparison a conventional tax or flat tax can be assumed to be 20%

PPR	PPR i-c function					
	PPR+0.25		PPR		PPR-0.25	
PPR	PPL%	net aY%	PPL%	net aY%	PPL%	net aY%
0.00	5.00%	95.00%	0.00%	100.00%	0.00%	100.00%
0.25	10.00%	90.00%	5.00%	95.00%	0.00%	100.00%
0.50	15.00%	85.00%	5.00%	95.00%	5.00%	95.00%
0.75	20.00%	80.00%	15.00%	85.00%	10.00%	90.00%
1.00	25.00%	75.00%	20.00%	80.00%	15.00%	85.00%
1.25	30.00%	70.00%	25.00%	75.00%	20.00%	80.00%

Key	Benefit		Flat tax		Prejudice	

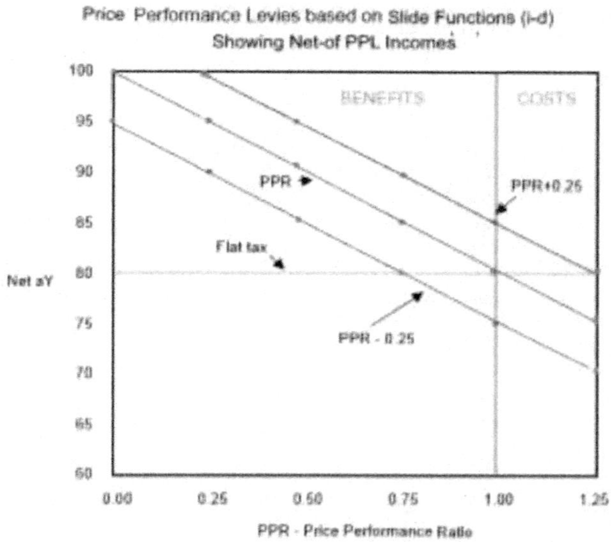

A note on conventional and flat taxes

In order to provide a comparison of the relative impacts of Price Performance Levy formulae and conventional and flat taxes, one can assume in the above tables that the flat tax is where the PPR values are ignored and the tax remains at 20%. The Real Incomes Approach sets out to compensate companies for their contribution to real incomes whereas flat taxes and conventional taxes are neutral to performance and pay no attention to the contribution of the company to the increase in real incomes. Accordingly, irrespective of the performance of a company, the tax rate remains the same. Thus, a company undergoing significant growth in nominal terms and generating a high return and profits might also be operating in a non-competitive fashion and in fact be a generator of inflation and contributing to the reduction in real incomes. This company will, under a flat tax regime, pay the same tax rate as a company investing and achieving higher performance in terms of contribution to real incomes.

Under 3P where the PPL is deployed, there is in fact no fixed corporate taxation, so the comparison with conventional and flat taxes does not really compare equivalent situations, but the advantage of 3P is evident. All revenues under 3P would normally come from personal taxation requiring, of course, reasonable rates of pay for employees made feasible by the more efficient allocation of resources and real income generation.

Under a Price Performance Policy, the benefits accruing to companies who contribute to real income levels can be observed in the tables above and the accompanying graphs. Under the flat tax, the net of tax is the remaining 80% of income. In the case of 3P ,net of tax income can vary from 80%-100% of gross income, that is levies of between 0% and 20% for PPRs below unity (<1.00).

Where the PPR is greater than unity (>1.00), the flat tax remains the same with a net income of 80% of gross, but under RIP, the levy becomes a surcharge leaving, in the examples above, net incomes of 61% to 80%.

The price-setting objectives under RIP encourage companies to set prices in order to pay a PPL at a rate tending towards or attaining zero (0%).

Annex 4
Public services and shadow pricing

In terms of accounts, it would be the response in aggregate unit costs to rises in aggregate unit costs that would be used to measure performance as a Costs Performance Ratio (CPR) as follows:

$$CPR = dAUC_2/dAUC_1$$

Where:

$dAUC_2$ is the response in aggregate unit costs to $dAUC_1$ where $dAUC_1$ is the rise in aggregate unit costs

The original shadow-PPR would be of the following form.
$sPPR = d(AUC_2 + M)/dAUC_1$

Where:

M is a nominal margin; $d(AUC_2 + M)$ is dUP applied in the original PPR formula
$dAUC_1$ is the rise in aggregate unit costs

Annex 5
Extension systems

Extension systems combine the functions of the collection of information on sector processes, technologies and techniques and analyses from the standpoint of costs, economic and operational efficiency and convenience and average contributions to margins or profits (gross margins) to create benchmarks of the state of the art of achievable performance generally classified into three practice categories of high, average and low or good or best, average or poor practice.

The central function of the extension system, in addition to this analysis and reporting based on data sets collected through sample surveys of sector participants, is the dissemination of this information through media and demonstrations including field demonstrations on the basis of an advisory function including training. The overall objective of extension systems is to sustain a constant flow of information and knowledge on the state of the art of sector technologies and techniques as a basis for sector participants to evaluate their own performance with what is feasible.

Where operators find that their practice is below average or indeed the best practice, the extension service data can usually indicate the gaps in their system or inputs causing the productivity deficit.

…

An Agricultural Innovation & Economic Development System

The central role of extension services

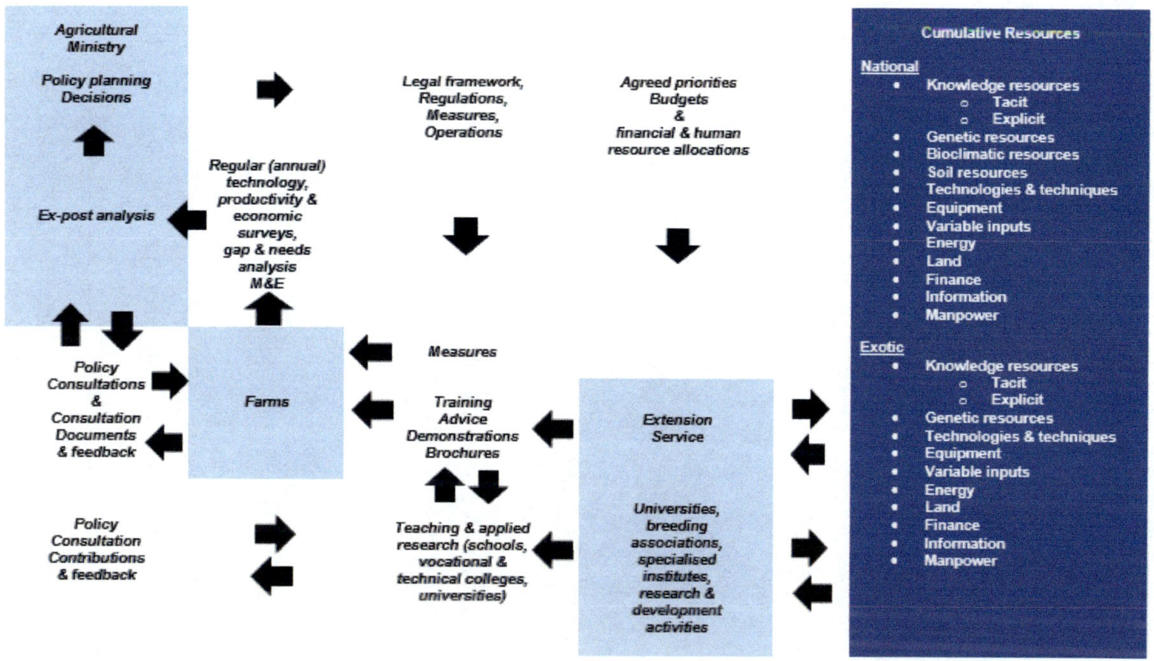

Source: McNeill, H. W., *"An Agricultural Innovation & Economic Development System AIEDS"*, SEEL, 2016

& Part 4: "*Impact analysis - why are so many project results disappointing?*", Agricultural Innovation, July,2020.

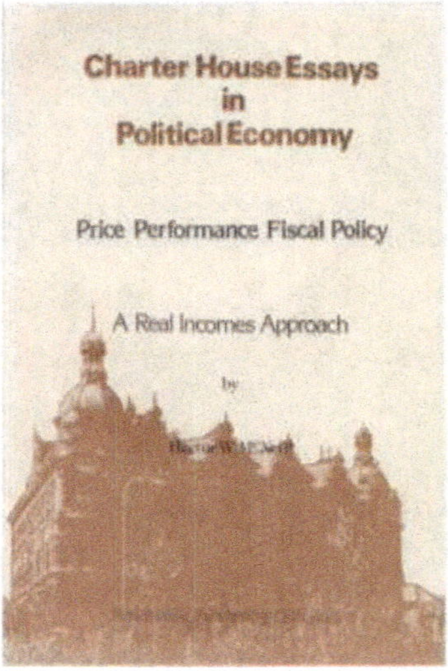

Early feedback received on 3P

On the left is the cover of the 1981 monograph [97] on 3P, circulated to British political parties. This was also the first edition of the series *Charter House Essays in Political Economy*

The first version of 3P was produced in 1976[96] in Rio de Janeiro where I made use of the Library of the Getúlio Vargas Foundation in Botafogo Bay.

In 1981, feedback on a monograph of 3P resulted in useful suggestions.

Robin Matthews, Professor of Economics at Cambridge University, while considering the system to work for

---

[97] McNeill, H. W, "., "*Price Performance Fiscal Policy – A Real Incomes Approach*", Charter House Essays in Political Economy, 1981. [96] McNeill, H. W., "*Price Performance Fiscal Policy – A Real Incomes Approach*", INTERCOMEX LTDA, Rio de Janeiro, June, 1976.

inflationary conditions, suggested that the PPR formula I had proposed needed to be adjusted to explore what would happen under deflationary conditions. At that time, the analysis only assumed rising inflation, the condition under stagflation when I started this work in 1975.

I therefore added the alternative PPR formula for deflationary conditions.

This had the effect of transforming 3P into a general macroeconomic policy, whereas the original version only addressed inflationary conditions.

I met with groups from the main political parties, but Labour was in turmoil because of the creation of the Social Democratic Party by four leading Labour MPs, and I ended up being advised to speak with the Trade Union Congress (TUC). In a meeting with Len Murray, the General Secretary of the TUC, it was obvious the monograph had not been read and Len Murray was unwilling to discuss anything that had not been vetted by the TUC.

As a result, there was no receptivity.

Lord Harry Renwick arranged meetings with people from the Conservative party, among which a senior manager from KPMG audit and management consultancy gave positive feedback stating he thought the proposition would work, but he advised me that at that time companies did not collect the type of information required to run such a scheme.

So, my thoughts on this matter were directed to the need for an information management system to facilitate this data collection.

A senior economics representative politician from the party, who happened to have attended the same university college as the author, I think, had not read the monograph, did not believe the policy could achieve a growth rate in excess of 1% and stuck on that point.

If he had read the monograph, he would have seen the methodology for the calculation.

It was clear that monetarism and supply-side economics had come to dominate economic thinking as the flavour of the period, filtering out just about anything that appeared to be different.

In reality, the only person, in addition to Robin Matthews, who appeared to have read and understood the monograph by the nature of his questions, was Richard Wainwright, the economic spokesman for the Liberal Party. He stated that he was positively impressed by the proposal and commented on the challenge of introducing and administering it. He stated:

"If we put that in our manifesto and we win, we would then be faced with the challenge of implementing it!"

At the time, he was right, because I had not turned my attention to the issue of implementation. Given the nature of 3P at that time, the capabilities of information technology and communications were not really adequate to handle the job. Most companies would not have had the required information technology devices. However, in the following 44 years, I addressed these issues and was greatly assisted by the revolution in information technology in the form of Structured Query Language (SQL) databases, personal computers, then laptops, Object Oriented Programming (OOP), standardized JavaScript and many other scripts, including Open Source, and the post-mid-1990s explosion in online capabilities and online systems.

Today, it is well within the capabilities of information technology and communications to manage 3P at the individual corporate level and the level of the government administration as set out in Part 6.

The Author:

Hector Wetherell McNeill

Hector Wetherell McNeill was born in Portsmouth, Hampshire, and attended Friends' School Great Ayton in North Yorkshire and the Southern Grammar School in Portsmouth.

He was a member of Clare College Cambridge reading the Agricultural Tripos at the School of Agriculture and subsequently post-graduate economics at the Faculty of Economics.

He was a Fellow of the Food Research Institute at Stanford University completing economics courses at the Department of Economics and systems engineering at the Engineering

School related to satellite based natural resources information collection and analysis and marine systems.

Soon after leaving Stanford, he initiated the development work on the Real Incomes Approach to Economics in 1975 in the midst of the global stagflation crisis. He started this enquiry as soon as he realized that conventional theory and policies could not solve stagflation without imposing prejudice on business and constituents.

He has dedicated almost 50 years to the development of the Real Incomes Approach to Economics and remains the main international exponent of this distinct school of economic thought.

Hector is Director of The George Boole Foundation Limited, a leading decision analysis development centre, and he is the Coordinator of SEEL-Systems Engineering Economics Lab, the international centre for the development of the Real Incomes Approach to Economics. He set up SEEL in 1983.

He was the first remote sensing expert to be contracted by the Plant Production Division of the Food & Agriculture Organization of the United Nations, heading an all Brazilian team to design and implement the world's first fully automatic crop inventory system for coffee.

He was a Senior Scientific Officer with the Information Technology & Telecommunications Task Force (ITTTF) in Brussels, heading systems groups identifying promising application developments for learning systems for several economic sectors in the European Union based on the emerging global network technologies and the Internet. His own contributions to this work gave rise to the Locational

State Theory, an extension of the discipline of decision analysis.
At the ITTTF he introduced user panels as a key part of systems groups organised to identify promising new applications for information technologies.

He was the environmental economist for the G7 Brazilian Rainforest Trust Fund based at the World Bank in Washington.

Hector is a member of the Royal Economic Society.

He is married and has a daughter.

He is a keen follower of modern jazz, Brazilian music and in particular Bossa Nova, Portuguese Fado and Spanish Flamenco and their derivatives.

He is fluent in Portuguese and plays jazz harmonica

Printed in Great Britain
by Amazon

49614652R00129